HENRIK IBSEN. BJÖRN-STJERNE BJÖRNSON. CRITICAL STUDIES. BY GEORGE BRANDES

FROM THE LIBRARY OF PUHLYAKOVA DASHA

LONDON: WILLIAM HEINEMANN
MDCCCXCIX

CONTENTS

HENRIK IBSEN

AUTHORISED TRANSLATION

By JESSIE MUIR

REVISED, WITH AN INTRODUCTION

By WILLIAM ARCHER

INTRODUCTION

IT would be a mere impertinence on my part, at any rate in this place, to attempt any criticism of Dr. Brandes's criticism of Henrik Ibsen. All I have any desire or right to do is to emphasise what Dr. Brandes himself says in his preface as to the peculiar, perhaps unique, circumstances under which this book has come into existence. I can remember no other instance in which a great critic, having followed the work of a great poet from, practically, the outset of the poet's career, has made, so to speak, a journal of his impressions, and republished them at last, with no correction or modification of any moment, simply in the chronological order of their original appearance. This is what Dr. Brandes has done. His book is thus not a focussed appreciation of the whole of Ibsen by the whole of Brandes, if I may so express it, but rather a contemporaneously-noted record of the ever-developing relation, throughout more than thirty years, of these two remarkable minds. It might have for its title, not, perhaps, "Ibsen Day by Day," but certainly "Ibsen Phase by Phase;" and this, of course, implies "Brandes Phase by Phase" as well.

Here lies the special interest and peculiar value of the book. If the reader wishes to see Dr. Brandes's judgments in their true perspective, it is essential that he should place himself, in relation to each of the three essays, at the writer's standpoint in time. To assist him in doing so, I shall briefly summarise Henrik Ibsen's literary position at the three dates in question.

The "First Impression" was begun, Dr. Brandes tells us, in

1866, and finished in 1867. The works of Ibsen which Dr.
Brandes had before him in 1867 were these :—

> Catilina (1850).
> The Feast at Solhaug (1856).
> Lady Inger of Östraat (1857).
> The Vikings at Helgeland (1858).
> Love's Comedy (1862).
> The Pretenders (1864).
> Brand (1866).
> Peer Gynt (1867).

Ibsen had also written, in 1850, *The Hero's Grave*, in 1852, *St.
John's Night*, and in 1857, *Olaf Liliekrans ;* but none of these
were at that time published or known to Dr. Brandes. He subsequently read two of them in manuscript, and speaks of them in
his " Third Impression." The first four sections of the " First
Impression " were finished before the appearance of *Peer Gynt*.
The fifth section, dealing with *Peer Gynt*, may thus be regarded
practically as a contemporary criticism of " the book of the day."
It will be noted that in 1867 Ibsen had not written a single prose
play of modern life. He was totally unknown outside Scandinavia, and only a year had passed since he made his first decisive
success in Norway and Denmark with *Brand*. Even with the
Scandinavian public he was still, as it were, on his probation.
Dr. Brandes's essay was the first detailed study of his work by
any critic of authority.

The " Second Impression " dates from 1882. It covers what
may be called Ibsen's transition period. The plays published
between 1867 and 1882 are as follows :—

> The League of Youth (1869).
> Emperor and Galilean (1873).
> The Pillars of Society (1877).
> A Doll's House (1879).
> Ghosts (1881).

These dates indicate that the poet was, during part of this period,
hesitating as to the path his genius ought to pursue. From 1862

to 1869 he had produced a play every two years, except that *Peer Gynt*, by a miracle of productivity, followed close on the heels of *Brand*, with only one year's interval.   In 1869 he produced his first prose play of modern life, *The League of Youth ;* and then came a pause of four years, during which he published nothing.   It is true that when he again broke silence it was with the titanic double-drama, *Emperor and Galilean*, which implied, if that were all, an amount of historical study that might well have occupied an even longer interval.   But after the appearance of the " world-historic drama," another space of four years elapsed before he came forward, in 1877, with *The Pillars of Society*, his second prose play of modern life.   He had now definitely chosen his line of development, and before the date of the " Second Impression," he had taken two gigantic strides along his new path, in *A Doll's House* and *Ghosts*.   By this time his fame had spread beyond the limits of Scandinavia.   *The Pillars of Society* had at once become popular (as it is to this day) on the German stage, and had prepared the way for *A Doll's House*, which, while equally popular, had made a far deeper impression in intellectual circles.   Most of his earlier works, too, had been translated into German ; of *Brand*, indeed, there existed three or four trans- lations.   Outside Germany, however, Ibsen was little known at the date of the "Second Impression."   Mr. Gosse, it is true, had introduced him to English readers, but in the Latin countries his name had scarcely been heard.   He stood, when Dr. Brandes wrote, on the threshold of the world-wide fame upon which he was soon to enter.   *Ghosts*, the harbinger, as it may fairly be called, of the whole modern dramatic movement in Europe, had just been published, and had not had time to make its mark outside Scandinavia, where it had been received with a shriek of execration.   Dr. Brandes was one of the few critics who instantly perceived its greatness and significance. He said of it, in an article not here reproduced, that it was, if not the greatest achievement, at any rate the noblest action of the poet's career. I quote from memory, at a distance of eighteen years, but I believe my recollection is substantially accurate. There has seldom been a truer or more timely criticism.

The "Third Impression" belongs to the present year (1898). Since the appearance of the "Second Impression" Ibsen has added to the roll of his writings the following plays:—

> An Enemy of the People (1882).
> The Wild Duck (1884).
> Rosmersholm (1886).
> The Lady from the Sea (1888).
> Hedda Gabler (1890).
> The Master-Builder (1892).
> Little Eyolf (1894).
> John Gabriel Borkman (1896).

Having reminded the reader of the order of these works, I need do no more. It seemed desirable to define the position occupied by Ibsen at the dates of the earlier "Impressions"; his position at the present day is matter of common knowledge.

This book, then, may be regarded as in some sort a running commentary on Ibsen's spiritual development. The leading English, French, and German critics (Mr. Gosse and possibly one or two Germans excepted) knew nothing of Ibsen until the greater number of his works were already written, and then studied them in the mass, as it were, and for the most part in translations. Dr. Brandes, on the other hand, writing practically the same language as Ibsen's, has followed every step of his development from the moment when his genius attained anything like maturity. He approached the study of the poet's works with a perfectly free mind, neither overawed by a great ready-made reputation, nor warped into antagonism by sectarian mispraise. His criticism throughout is absolutely candid. In the "First Impression," indeed, it is so largely unfavourable that

the fact of their subsequent intimate friendship speaks volumes
for the character of both men. Many a lesser poet would have
resented for ever the critic's outspokenness. Ibsen, on the
contrary, not only entered into cordial personal relations with
his critic, but actually altered several passages (as will be seen
from the notes on pp. 23 and 30) in deference to Dr. Brandes's
judgment. During the 'seventies, Ibsen and Dr. Brandes were
in close correspondence; and the extracts from the poet's letters,
which appear in the "Second Impression," impart to it a peculiar interest and importance. In none of his plays has Ibsen
said anything weightier or more characteristic than the remark
(quoted on p. 56), "What is really wanted is a revolution of the
spirit of man "—*Menneskeaandens Revoltering*.

Dr. Brandes's book of *Ungdomsvers* ("Poems of Youth"), published a few months ago in Copenhagen, enables us to supplement
this utterance. We learn from the motto prefixed to an address "To Henrik Ibsen," that the poet added, "And in that
revolution *you* must be one of the leaders." Close as is the
friendship, however, indicated in this correspondence, no one
who reads the following pages can for a moment pretend that
it has impaired Dr. Brandes's independence of judgment. It is
no eulogy of Ibsen that is here presented to the English-speak-
ing public. Some admirers of the poet may think the critic, at
points, over-severe and perhaps even captious. Let them remember that absolute sincerity is of more importance than
absolute correctness, even if "correctness" could fitly be pre-
dicated of any æsthetic judgment. It is their complete unsec-
tarianism, even more than their delicacy of appreciation, that
leads me to regard these essays as of greater value than many
more exhaustive and pretentious critical studies of Ibsen that
have appeared in Swedish, German, and French. Here, and
here only, has a critical intelligence of the first order been
brought to bear, in detail, upon the poet's creations.

Passages quoted from *Brand* are given in Professor Herford's
translation (Heinemann, 1894); passages from *Peer Gynt*, in

the translation by my brother and myself, published by Walter Scott. Other metrical quotations, hitherto untranslated, I have rendered as best I might, since no other course seemed possible, but must beg the reader to remember that my versions do sad injustice to the poet's metrical style. Footnotes appended by Dr. Brandes are distinguished by his initials. For all others I am responsible.

WILLIAM ARCHER.

AUTHOR'S PREFACE

In the summer of 1866, after having been for some years interested in Henrik Ibsen's work, I wrote the first pages of this book; I could not, however, get on with the paper I was desirous of writing, and went to Paris. On my return, in 1867, I finished the paper, which was the earliest full-length picture of Ibsen's intellectual personality that had been attempted in Europe.

After an interval of between fifteen and sixteen years, I again, in 1882, returned to the Norwegian poet's personality and works. He had in the meantime developed greatly, and had produced a number of works that threw his earlier ones into the shade. He had become another and a greater man, and had gained extraordinary renown in Scandinavian countries, while his name had begun to penetrate into other lands, especially Germany. Neither in his inward nor in his outward circumstances was he now quite the same as at the time the first account of his poetic labours was given.

But neither was his critic quite the same. He had in the meantime gone through a great deal, and had consequently acquired a larger outlook upon life, and a more flexible emotional nature. He had dropped all the doctrines that were due to education and tradition. He understood the poet better now.

Once more sixteen years have passed. With the equable power that distinguishes him, Ibsen has continued his efforts without interruption, and during this time his fame has become world-wide. No living dramatist has a name to be compared with his. True, his position is contested, and his works are far from meeting with unanimous admiration; but he occupies the thoughts of all his contemporaries, and what more can a productive spirit require?

It is well known that Henrik Ibsen completed his seventieth year on the 20th March 1898. I have, in commemoration of this anniversary, combined my first and second essays upon him with a third, which brings my account of his poetic labours down to our own day. By a strange chance, I have happened, in the course of rather more than a generation, to discuss him thrice, at equal intervals of time. When I first wrote about him, he was between thirty-eight and thirty-nine, the second time fifty-four, and now he has lived to see a birthday that is remembered in all civilised countries, and celebrated in many.

Those who, in foreign countries, have discussed Henrik Ibsen's poetic career, have, as a rule, been able to make a general survey of it before they wrote. They have not read the works in the order, and at the intervals of time, in which they came into being; they have seen all the features of his physiognomy at once; they have had the whole fabric of his life-work before them, and have deduced from it, as it were, a more or less correct picture of the master-builder. It may at some future time be interesting to see how the building was reflected in the mind of a contemporary who saw it come into being, and who, at a comparatively early time, was so situated as to be able, from his impressions of the master-builder's personality, to say a few words of guidance to students of his work.

G. B.

FIRST IMPRESSION

(1867)

HENRIK IBSEN

FIRST IMPRESSION

(1867)

IT is by two polemical works that Henrik Ibsen's name has chiefly become known to the Danish reading public. Dissimilar as these are in respect of maturity and depth, they have, in combination, inevitably given the public the impression that Ibsen's nature is pre-eminently combative. In *Love's Comedy*, on behalf of beauty and poetry, in *Brand*, on behalf of morals and religion, he has declared war and gone out to battle against the entire existing social status — giving his attack, of course, a special reference to Norway. In both poems the struggle is tragic. According to Ibsen, neither uncompromising passion nor uncompromising will can co-exist with existing society. These spiritual forces must have air, and require room. Life has no room to spare, and to procure it they seek to revolutionise this society that lies rotting in stagnation. But the revolution does not end in reform; the "comedy" of love is really its tragedy, and the drama of will ends in a martyrdom.

Whatever the merits or defects of his productions, it is clear that we have here to deal with a poet who looks upon the life of the present day with the eye of a pessimist: not a pessimist in the sense—the philosophico-poetic sense—that melancholy is his muse, his work a lamentation over the hapless lot of humanity, and his inspiration a deep sense of the tragedy inherent in the mere fact of human existence; but a pessimist whose pessimism is of a moral character, akin to contempt and indignation. He does not bemoan, he indicts. His gloomy way of looking at things makes him, in the first place, polemical; for when he

3

directs his gaze towards his own time, it presents to his eye sheer
misery and guilt, and shows him the discord between what ought
to be and what is. In the second place, it makes him bitter; for
when he turns his gaze on the ideal, he sees its destruction as
inevitable, all higher living and striving as fruitless, and discord between what ought to be, and what is, attainable. There
is a revolutionary element in these works. But why should all
these revolutionary endeavours be represented as failures? One
possible answer is: because society has sunk far too low to allow
of its being raised; a second is: because the champion of the
truth is himself involved in injustice and guilt; a third: because
it is the destiny of truth and beauty only to shine forth for a
moment, like meteors that are extinguished as soon as they
touch the earth; a fourth: because in Henrik Ibsen's poetic
spirit there is a peculiar bias that forces him to depict life in
just this manner. In the last analysis, however, there is no
other answer than that he represents life as it presents itself
to him; that there is probably something in the innermost recesses of his nature that compels him to represent and depict
life as a mighty but despairing struggle up towards the good;
something in his eye that makes his outlook black; something
combative, rebellious, violent, and melancholy deep down in his
being that is reflected in his works, and darkens even his love
for the light.

The correctness of this supposition may be put to the test.
If we wish to discover a secret, we observe the person concerned
in an unguarded moment, when he is unconsciously revealing his
innermost thought. The prisoner is aroused from slumber to
be examined; he betrays himself most easily in the moment of
awakening. Thus is it with the poetic individuality; as it awakes,
it catches involuntarily at a subject, a form, a personality, through
which it can express itself and obtain a hearing. Ibsen's first
poetic attempt, made while he was yet poring over his Sallust at
school, a grown-up scholar, backward in his studies but forward
in development, is a drama in which he, like Schiller in *The
Robbers*, has given vent to all the passion that can seethe in
a young, untried heart, boiling over with the wrath and love,
despair and ambitious self-esteem, of twenty years. Who do
you think is the hero of this boyish and immature production?
No other than that *enfant perdu* of Roman society, to whose

unbridled audacity and unparalleled foolhardiness we owe our
first impressions of Ciceronian eloquence and our first knowledge of Latin syntax—in a word, Catiline.   He is represented
as a heroic figure, a colossal and potent spirit, held, it is true,
in the grasp of mean instincts, but created for some great end,
towering up above his wretched, depraved associates in a miserable period of decadence, a " desperado " like Falk and Brand,
who, in his burning enthusiasm for the grandeur of olden
days, raises the banner of revolution, and falls a victim partly to
treachery, partly to his own guilt, which he expiates in death.
Thus, even here, we already find the same pessimism (in the
view of Roman society), the same combative spirit, the same
overflowing pathos, the same desperate butting against a stone
wall.

The main impression, then, of this poet, which has been
received in Denmark, appears, although certainly one-sided, to
be essentially correct ; and when we look at the facts that are
known about his life, we find that they too are in keeping with
his poetic character.   We can understand that a life like his may
have contributed to give to mental capacities of this magnitude
just that peculiar stamp which the poems exhibit.

Henrik Ibsen was born on the 20th March 1828, at Skien,
in Norway, and in his sixteenth year was apprenticed to a
chemist, but was seized with a desire to study medicine, and
prepared himself, in spite of difficulties, for his matriculation
examination.   He was twenty-two when he passed it, and had
by that time " neither the means nor the desire " for professional
study.   His circumstances were wretched ; for some time he
could not even afford to dine regularly.   His youth was thus
severe and hard ; as a young man he did not see the bright side
of existence, and his own life was not only an inward but an
outward struggle.   The transition is easy from hardness and
severity to fierceness, passionateness, and irregularity.

In 1850 *Catilina* appeared.   In 1851 Ibsen began to edit a
weekly paper, for which he wrote lyrical and satirical pieces.   In
the same year he was appointed stage manager of the newly
opened theatre in Bergen, and in 1852 he paid a short visit to
Denmark and Germany to study their theatres.   In 1857 he became artistic director of the Norwegian Theatre in Christiania, and
in the following year he married his present wife, a step-daughter

of the authoress, Magdalene Thoresen. The theatre having
failed in 1862, Ibsen, after some time, left Norway, and since
then has generally lived in Rome. Before his departure he had
written a number of lyrical poems and a series of dramas. During
his connection with the theatre in Norway, he was the object of
constant attacks from the press; and he seems on the whole to
be continually at war with his countrymen (see, for example, the
preface to the second edition of *Love's Comedy*). At home he
had been obliged to struggle with poverty; it was commonly
reported that in Rome he was in actual want at the time when
Brand appeared in Copenhagen.

That book marked the turning-point in his fate. As every
one is aware, the work, or rather its hero—for the idea of the
poem is not clear—preaches the doctrine that one should cast off
all worldly cares. The Norwegian people, with a delicacy of
consideration (and, apparently at least, of irony) with which
few, perhaps, would have credited them, showed that they
appreciated the possession of a man, who, in the present day,
proclaimed truths such as these. They desired that this man,
freed from the petty cares of bread-winning, should continue
to proclaim so elevated a view. The Norwegian Storthing voted
Ibsen an annual grant, and thus a modest competency has fortunately been assured to the poet for the future.[1]

[1] It appears from Jæger's biography of Ibsen (translated by Miss Clara Bell,
1890) that the government had granted him a "travelling stipend" before he left
Norway. Oddly enough, it was paid him by the "Ecclesiastical Department."

I

THAT which above all interests us in a poet of the present day is the new thought that comes to life in him. Our first question is: " Where lies his discovery? what is his America? " For a single great new poetical discovery we will forgive him much; but if he is to gain admission to our sympathy and admiration, he must first of all be able to point to such an one. Our whole interest in modern Norwegian literature is dependent upon this easily explained circumstance. Nothing is more certain than that Norwegian poetry, as regards rounded harmonious form, purity of style, the repose which many-sided culture alone gives to a poet's work, is far inferior to the poetry which in Denmark concludes an important literary period, rich in all forms and branches of poetic art. How great a leap it seems, how deep a fall, from the classical finish of expression in Heiberg's or Paludan-Müller's best poems, and Fru Gyllembourg's novels, to the mannerism of Björnson's earlier plays, or Fru Thoresen's strained and laboured prose. And yet every one prefers these works to the ephemeral aftermath which appeared in Norway as the immediate continuation of our own literary movement. Although Norway needed Denmark as an interpreter and mediator between herself and Europe, although the common literature of the two countries has given Norway her training and her artistic models, yet what we Danes especially value and enjoy in Norwegian literature is, of course, that which appears as the beginning of a new and independent life. The first requisite for the awakening of our sister-country's powers was that the flood of culture should flow so far north that from Denmark it could spread with fertilising power over Norway; the next that, on the separation of Norway from Denmark, and her consequent attainment of independence and political freedom, this same flood should retreat, leaving behind it its fertilising deposit. The poetical growth which then shot up has attained its most delicate and beautiful development in the story, in Björnson's peasant-novels, but its highest significance in the serious historical play.

Where now in Ibsen shall we seek for the new thought? The Danish public have learnt to know him as a polemist. If he were nothing more, we could found no great hopes on him as a poet; a merely destructive spirit is not a poetical one. It is true that every No contains a Yes; it is true that in poetry something new and original may once in a way appear in the form of a negative; but this has not been the case in the present instance. We shall endeavour to prove this assertion later on, and in the meantime turn, as we naturally must, to Ibsen's positive productions, his other dramas.[1] If, however, we read these in their chronological order, and come to them with considerable expectations, we shall most certainly be surprised and disappointed. We may read on and on without being struck by any new idea, without being impressed by any new poetic vision. To tell the plain truth, Henrik Ibsen has produced only one single drama that is at the same time original and, in spite of faults in detail, thoroughly successful; but that one is of such importance, that it insures him a high place among the poetic spirits of the north.

Henrik Ibsen is not one of the happy poets. A happy poet is one who early, if not at once, discovers in himself a peculiar fund of matter, of new themes, and, with each theme, a beautiful and clear expression for everything that at that stage of his development he is able to express. Such a poet will probably, in course of time, be able to produce more important works than his first, and, in accordance with the progress of his mind, he will be able frequently to change the form or style of his art; but each of his works will be perfect of its kind, the less as well as the greater, and they will all, in spite of their differences, have two things in common—the impress of beauty and of the poet's own spirit. It is not so with Ibsen's plays and poems. He makes start after start, each, as it were, the run before the leap that is to carry him into his promised land. But for a long time it seemed as though this leap would never be taken. His genius cannot come to rest; it tosses about like a sick, restless child; now it searches within among its dreams and thoughts, but does not find them clear or strong enough to be able to step

---

[1] Other than *Love's Comedy* and *Brand*, that is to say, which Dr. Brandes classes as polemical and negative.

forth in vigorous nudity; now it searches without, finds a delicate, spotless drapery, wraps itself in it so as to become almost unrecognisable, seeks for a style, nay more, a language; then it throws away what it has found, realises at length that all borrowing is pure loss, and labours until at last it finds its true self.

Ibsen found himself when, after having written his two prentice works, *Catilina*, in Danish iambic pentameters, and *The Feast at Solhaug*, in old ballad metre,[1] he wrote, in 1857, for the Christiania theatre, *Lady Inger of Östraat*, a historical tragedy in prose, and in the year following, 1858, *The Vikings at Helgeland*, a dramatic adaptation of the ancient legend of the Völsungs. Both of these are interesting works, the former especially so, although neither possesses that strongly-marked originality which we subsequently find in him. Their individuality lies at any rate only in their style and manner of presentation, which strive more and more towards the attainment of grandeur and power, and not in their ideas, which strike us as familiar, and which we seem to have met with before, if nowhere else, at least in the poet himself. He has a peculiar propensity for varying the same motives. He goes ever farther and farther into the depths—this is indeed the law of his progress—but enlarges his horizon less rapidly. His is rather a deep than a comprehensive spirit. And he does not easily overcome his adaptive tendency. We still find it in the last of these works, *The Vikings*, which is indeed a new conquest, but like so many conquests, associated with very extensive plundering. In order to gather characteristic and lively traits of ancient life for his play, Ibsen has picked out effective bits from many different songs and legends, and, as Goldschmidt once aptly expressed it, has actually "scoured" the old sagas. When he is not adapting from others, he adapts from himself. Look at his characters, for instance. He is like the artist who always employs the same model; seated he is Brutus, standing, Christian IV.; in a chiton he is Achilles, nude, he is Samson. It is a great convenience for a poet to be what in former times was called *subjective*, for then he has always his model at hand. In *Lady Inger of Östraat*, we find Ibsen's favourite type, with peculiar qualities, but still easily recognisable. Vaguely, and in the widest signification of the words, this type may be characterised as "the very devil of a fellow," an expression which may be understood in both a good and

---

[1] And partly in prose.

a bad sense. The principal male character in *Lady Inger* is the Danish knight, Nils Lykke, a man, as his name[1] presages, *à bonnes fortunes*, a Don Juan approaching middle age, like Catiline irresistible, ambitious, and highly talented. As though to complete the analogy, the poet has utilised afresh the fundamental motive of *Catilina*, the punishment of the tardily converted libertine through a love-affair with a girl who loathes and curses him, because he has brought dishonour upon her sister, and laid her in her grave. As with the characters, so with the relations in which they stand—Ibsen reverts again and again to the same conjuncture.

He delights in placing a strong, richly endowed, fully developed masculine nature between two women, one fierce and the other mild, one a mannish valkyrie or fury, and the other tender, lovable, and of womanly gentleness. Thus he placed Catiline between the terrible Furia and the gentle Aurelia, his wife and guardian angel; thus he places Gudmund, in *The Feast at Solhaug*, between the "Ragnhild" and "Regisse"[2] of the play; and thus, in *The Vikings*, he places the Sigurd of the legend between Brynhild and Gudrun, or, as they are here called, Hjördis and Dagny. In the same manner he afterwards places Brand between the wild woman, Gerd, his evil genius, and his wife, the delicate and feminine Agnes.

In opposition and contrast to his hero, he then sets up a weak, subordinate, masculine character, first caricatured as Bengt in *The Feast at Solhaug*, but subsequently acquiring more and more importance, and developing into the honourably human, the prosaically estimable man, who stands to the demigod or hero as the commonplace character to the genius—a *beta* who can never become an *alpha*. Thus in *The Vikings* we find the brave, honest Gunnar opposed to the romantic hero Sigurd, who does not indeed, as in the legend, ride through the fire, but does fight with the bear; and thus, afterwards, in *Love's Comedy*, Guldstad, the sensible merchant and good husband (to be) is opposed to the ideal Pegasus-rider, Falk. But the one has the labour, the other the reward. It is Gunnar and Guldstad, the pedestrian pair, who win the two enchanted princesses whom the knights on horse-

---

[1] "Lykke" means luck or good fortune. The name, however, is historical.

[2] Characters in Henrik Hertz's *Svend Dyring's House*. As to the relation between this play and *The Feast at Solhaug*, see pp. 49 and 89.

back rescued. Even a Völsung name is found in the modern poem: the heroine is called Svanhild, and the legendary associations of the name are dwelt upon.

It cannot be denied that this poet puts his talent out at usance; but we take a mistaken view of the matter if we see nothing more in it than this; for what is this circling around the same fundamental thoughts, this deepening of the same tracks, and this incredible obstinacy in investigating a narrow range of great fundamental relations—what is it but the poet's ever deeper absorption in himself? One feels how he digs down into his own inner being, and, like the treasure-seeker, little by little loses interest in every other treasure than the one he is in search of. And is he not always getting closer to it? The dullest reader who compares these works will see that each fresh one means an advance, that with each one of them Ibsen has gone a step, if not farther, at any rate deeper.

It is not difficult to place our finger on the interest which directs his choice precisely to these subjects. One can see what it is that attracts his mind, as by ties of kinship. We here find our polemist once more. His ideal, like that of other recent Norwegian poets, is one made up of greatness and strength, of passion and will, and of will upborne by passion; but it imposes a polemical attitude towards his contemporaries upon this poet, who has never, like the writers of the peasant-story, attempted to depict a vigorous present-day life. Strength of will is to him the really sublime; it is that around which his thoughts again circle in *Brand*, just as purity of will is always, for Paludan-Müller, the centre around which everything turns.

Again, we find in all Ibsen's works the polemical poet's taste for the tragical, and the restless melancholy by virtue of which he seeks intensely thrilling incidents, and terrible, paralysing situations, in which great strength is wasted to no purpose. Take a single instance: in *Lady Inger*, the protagonist is a woman of rare intellectual powers, placed in a high position, at the head of her people, with all eyes resting upon her. She is born to be the leader of this people's revolt, born to be their deliverer from the dominion of tyrants. The sacredness of the cause, the enthusiasm of her soul, her wisdom, her courage, the vows of her youth, everything combines to incite or compel her to act and conquer. But she is unable to stir, she dare not lift a hand, for a son, the fruit of a secret, unlawful attachment, is a hostage in the enemies' power. Her fear for his life paralyses her all her life through, and at last she herself has him murdered, taking him for another, and believing that this crime will save him, and pave his way to the Norwegian throne. Like Hjördis in *The Vikings*, she is most cruel to him she loves best. A situation such as that in which this woman is placed calls to mind Puget's famous group of Milo defending himself against the attack of the lion, but writhing in vain, without being able to use his mighty strength; for while one hand is in the lion's mouth, the other is held fast in a cloven tree, whence it is impossible for him to wrench it loose.

Lastly, we find here, where nothing is entirely good, but where powerful pathos, flashes of great thoughts, and a high reflectiveness are never lacking, the same fundamental principle which we learned to know in the polemical poems. There we saw it as sparks from the fire of enthusiasm, and heard it as the crack of the spirit's whip. But neither there nor here do we find a single, tranquil stream flowing direct from Nature's spring.

II

THEN comes *The Pretenders*. The play appeared in 1864, and thus stands between the two polemical poems. And what is it that *The Pretenders* treats of? Looked at simply, it is an old story. We all know the story of Aladdin and Nureddin, the simple legend in the "Arabian Nights," and our great poet's [1] incomparable poem. In *The Pretenders* two figures again stand opposed to one another as the superior and the inferior being, an Aladdin and a Nureddin nature; for it was towards this contrast, with which the poetry of the century begins here in the North,[2] that Ibsen had hitherto unconsciously directed his endeavours, just as Nature feels her way in her blind, preliminary attempts to form her types. Hakon and Skule are pretenders to the same throne, scions of royalty out of whom a king may be made. But the first is the incarnation of fortune, victory, right, and confidence, the second —the principal figure of the play, masterly in its truth and originality—is the brooder, a prey to inward struggle and endless distrust, brave and ambitious, with perhaps every qualification and claim to be king, but lacking the inexpressible, impalpable somewhat that would give a value to all the rest—the wonderful lamp. "I am a king's arm," he says, "mayhap a king's brain as well; but Hakon is the whole king." "You have wisdom and courage, and all noble gifts of the mind," says Hakon to him; "you are born to stand nearest a king, but not to be a king yourself."

With Hakon the very reverse is the case. He is no abler than the bishop, no bolder than Skule, but yet he is the greatest man. For who is the greatest man? "The boldest," says the warrior; "the man of greatest faith," says the priest; but Bishop Nicolas explains that it is neither of these :—

---

[1] The Danish poet, Oehlenschläger.
[2] Oehlenschläger's *Aladdin* appeared in 1805.

"The most fortunate man [1] is the greatest man.   It is the most fortunate man that does the greatest deeds—he whom the cravings of his time seize like a passion, begetting thoughts he himself cannot fathom, and pointing to paths which lead he knows not whither, but which he follows and must follow till he hears the people shout for joy, and, looking around him with wondering eyes, finds himself the hero of a great achievement."

So fortunate is Hakon.   "Does not everything thrive with him?" cries Skule:—

"Does not everything shape itself for the best, when he is concerned? Even the peasants note it; they say the trees bear fruit twice, and the birds hatch out two broods every summer, whilst Hakon is king. Vermeland, where he burned and harried, stands smiling with its houses built afresh, and its cornlands bending heavy-eared before the breeze. 'Tis as though blood and ashes fertilised the land where Hakon's armies pass; 'tis as though the Lord clothed with double verdure what Hakon had trampled down; 'tis as though the holy powers made haste to blot out all evil in his track.   And how easy has been his path to the throne!   He needed that Inge should die early, and Inge died: his youth needed to be watched and warded, and his men kept watch and ward around him; he needed the ordeal, and his mother bore the iron for him."

What an Aladdin!   And yet he is something far more than, something quite different from, Aladdin; half a century lies between him and Aladdin.[2]   He is more than the victorious favourite of fortune, whose desire is one with its fulfilment, and whose behests are always obeyed.   He has something besides and beyond good fortune, something stronger and higher than good fortune, which therefore raises him above Aladdin.   This something we may for the present designate as the right.   Right has no place in Aladdin's sphere; when Aladdin is right, it is only because he cannot be wrong.   A concept so remote from unsophisticated nature as "right," a concept so entirely the product of reflection, so inseparable from civilisation and reality, could only by an error on the poet's part be brought into relation to Aladdin.

[1] *Den lykkeligste mand.*   The word *lykke* means not only luck or fortune, but happiness.   To render *lykkeligste* completely, we should require a word in which the ideas "fortunate" and "happy" should be blent.

[2] Again, of course, an allusion to Oehlenschläger's hero.

Right is the outward manifestation of the good in a community; not indeed the good itself, but its exterior aspect. The moral idea, however, is far too fixed and hard to allow of its finding a place in a poem like *Aladdin;* it tears the poem to pieces wherever it is thrown in, as a stone tears a fine, fluttering tissue of threads. Heiberg has made this remark: "The moral idea is too heavy for the fairy-like, fantastic material that does not yet . . . know the difference between good and evil." But in *The Pretenders* we are within the historic domain, and have the firm ground of reality beneath our feet. The taste for the historical in our day has succeeded to the bias in the immediate past towards the symbolic-ideal; the partiality for the strictly-ethical (sometimes also for the narrowly-pietistic) has supplanted the worship of beauty; sympathy has turned from spiritual symbolism to the life of action and achievement. Fortune is a concept belonging to the purely natural way of regarding life; right carries us at once into the ethical sphere. That speech, therefore, is a most profound one, in which the evil genius of the play attempts, by a single word, to subordinate the moral to the purely natural point of view.

"The right is Hakon's, Bishop," says Skule; and the Bishop replies: "The right is his, for he is the fortunate one; *'tis even the summit of fortune, to have the right. But by what right has Hakon the right, and not you?*" What an utterance! What depths must there not be in the mind of the poet who can conceive a thing like that! At a single turn of the wrist, in a flash so rapid that the eye can scarcely follow it, Morality is thrown at the feet of Nature, the ethical dissolved in the metaphysical. "With what right did he obtain the right?" This question is an attempt to get behind Morality, to attack it in the rear, kill it from behind. But the feat cannot be thus achieved. Morality puts on double strength, for the very question that would evade right employs the word "right." This one speech affords us a measure of the progress from Oehlenschläger's period to Ibsen's.

But we said that right was only a provisional designation for the something which Hakon possesses over and above the gifts of Aladdin. It is even possible that he has not the formal right at all. "But," exclaims Skule, "*he himself* believes it—*that* is the heart of his fortune, *that* is the girdle of strength." One feels that Ibsen has rated at its true value the high confidence and

unswerving faith with which Hakon knows in his own soul that
he is the rightful heir.   It is upon healthy self-reliance, that ideal
towards which the present generation aspires with longing and
struggling, and upon self-distrust, the gnawing worm of the age,
that the whole drama turns as upon its axis.   The poet has given
us in Skule's monologues a masterly analysis of the restlessness
and tortures of self-mistrust.   What are Nureddin's broodings
and doubts compared with this struggle?   Nureddin is not a
person, not a soul, but a symbol.   All Skule's struggles are solitary wrestlings of his personality with itself, the fight to gain
faith, not in a supernatural, but in a natural sense.

The last, rather too personal, testimonial which Ibsen received
from Norway before he wrote *The-Pretenders*, was the remark in his
biography, written by a friend in the *Norsk Illustreret Nyhedsblad*,
that with all his gifts, he "lacked ideal faith and conviction."   Be
this as it may, Ibsen seems to have taken this very failing as his
problem; and it is evident that if it entered into his character, he
at least did not harbour it as a stranger, unknown to himself.

Certain though it be that Skule is an inferior nature, it is impossible for him to rest content with this thought.   His boundless
ambition cannot brook the idea that he has a superior.   Hakon
must share the power with him.   "I am soul-sick, and there is
no other healing for me.   We two must be equals; there must be
no man over me."   Power he must have on any terms.   He calls
upon Hakon to divide the kingdom with him, or to take turns
with him in ruling; he challenges him to single combat for the
supremacy; he has staked his life on this thing.   It is then that
Hakon's answer completely crushes him.   Hakon's is no empty
confidence; it rests upon an idea, on a thought for the future.

"*Hakon.* I was young and untried when I came to the helm—look
at me—all fell before me when I became king; there are no Baglers,
no Ribbungs left!

"*Duke Skule.* That should you least boast of; for there lies the
greatest danger.   Party must stand against party, claim against claim,
region against region, if the king is to have the might.   Every village,
every family must either need him or fear him.   If you kill dissension,
you kill your power at the same stroke.

"*Hakon.* And you would be king—you, who think thus!   You had
been well enough fitted for a chieftain's part in Erling Skakke's days;
but the time has grown away from you, and you know it not.   See you

not, then, that Norway's realm, as Harald and Olaf built it up, may be likened to a church that stands as yet unconsecrate? The walls soar aloft with mighty buttresses, the vaultings have a noble span, the spire points upwards, like a fir-tree in the forest; but the life, the throbbing heart, the fresh blood-stream, is lacking to the work; God's living spirit is not breathed into it; it stands unconsecrate. *I* will bring consecration! Norway has been a *kingdom*, it shall become a *people*. The Trönder has stood against the man of Viken, the Agdeman against the Hordalander, the Halogalander against the Sogndalesman; all shall be one hereafter, and all shall feel and know that they are one!

"*Duke Skule* (*impressed*). To unite—— ? To unite the Trönders and the men of Viken—all Norway—— ? (*Incredulously.*) 'Tis impossible! Norway's saga tells of no such thing!

"*Hakon.* For you 'tis impossible, for you can but work out the old saga afresh; for me, 'tis as easy as for the falcon to cleave the clouds."

This scene is certainly one of the most clearly conceived and most deeply felt that any dramatic literature can exhibit.

After this spiritual defeat, Skule conceives the idea of appropriating Hakon's thought and putting it into action. With this end in view, he has himself proclaimed king. It is Nureddin stealing Aladdin's lamp. He fights, and to his own astonishment wins; but even after the victory he trembles, and scarcely dares to believe in the possibility of the event which he knows to be an accomplished fact. Thus stands Nureddin with trembling knees, the lamp falling from his hand, at the very moment when the genie appears, prepared to obey him unconditionally.

If Skule has no belief in himself, he feels, on the other hand, the deepest, most burning desire to have near him some one who fully and absolutely believes in him, so that he may draw strength from the other's confidence. For some time he seeks in vain. Then the beloved of his youth brings him his son, and in this son he finds what he seeks: limitless admiration, and a filial devotion that is ready to believe everything. The son seizes upon the "king's thought," understands its greatness, and consecrates his life to its realisation. But henceforth the curse of guilt is upon Skule. All his battles end in defeat; and his conscience is yet further burdened when his son, carried away by fanaticism, overleaps all barriers, and commits sacrilege. Then it is that at length, deeply humbled, he strips himself of all his borrowed splendour, and confesses to his son that the "king's

B

thought" was Hakon's. And then he dies, reconciled to his fate, together with his son.

When we are really touched by a poem, it is generally because we silently transmute its substance into such forms as come home to us intimately, familiarly. We translate it from its own language into our personal mother-tongue. We are affected by Paludan-Müller's *Cain*, although none of us has committed fratricide. But it is not of fratricide that we think as we read it. This is the case, too, with the poet himself: he has often a more intimate personal understanding of his work than that which it directly suggests. In *The Pretenders* there is a masterly scene between Skule and the skald whom he wishes to make his friend.

"*King Skule.* Have you many unsung songs within you, Jatgeir?

"*Jatgeir.* Nay, but many unborn; they are conceived one after the other, come to life, and are brought forth.

"*King Skule.* And if I, who am king and have the might, if I were to have you slain, would all the unborn skald-thoughts you bear within you die along with you?

"*Jatgeir.* My lord, it is a great sin to slay a fair thought.

"*King Skule.* I ask not if it be a *sin;* I ask if it be *possible!*

"*Jatgeir.* I know not.

"*King Skule.* Have you never had another skald for your friend, and has he never unfolded to you a great and noble song he thought to make?

"*Jatgeir.* Yes, lord.

"*King Skule.* Did you not then wish that you could slay him, to take his thought and make the song yourself?

"*Jatgeir.* My lord, I am not barren; I have children of my own. I need not to love those of other men.

.   .   .   .

"*King Skule* (*seizes him by the arm*). What gift do I need to become a king?

"*Jatgeir.* Not the gift of doubt; else would you not question so.

"*King Skule.* What gift do I need?

"*Jatgeir.* My lord, you *are* a king.

"*King Skule.* Have *you* at all times full faith that you are a *skald?*"

How much this speech implies! It reverses the situation so that the image becomes the substance and the substance the image. What a painful confession lies in those last words: " Have you at all times full faith that you are a skald?"

The same idea of a spirit yearning to rise higher than its powers permit, is presented under another guise in the monster, Bishop Nicolas, whose great energies have been wasted in sheer impotent coveting and craving. Notwithstanding the fact of this variation, however, Ibsen cannot, if we have rightly interpreted the natural bent of his mind, have attained all at once to the conception of Skule and his entanglements. The tragic situation of such a figure cannot all at once have presented itself to him in such purity and grandeur. He must have made preliminary attempts, must have modelled and grouped the figures in clay before he chiselled them out in marble. Let us look back at *The Vikings in Helgeland.* What attracted Ibsen to the mythic cycle in general was, no doubt, its wildness and grandeur; but he chose this particular theme on account of the peculiar character of the tragic conflict it presents. As we know, it is Sigurd who, in Gunnar's armour, has slain the bear, and won Hjördis; but no one suspects this, and, noble and blameless as Gunnar is, he has to conceal the truth, bear the burden of honour for an exploit that he has never performed or been capable of performing, and listen to praises of his deed which, in Sigurd's presence, sound to him worse than the bitterest contempt. As Skule is the plagiarist of an idea, so Gunnar is the robber of an achievement, and it is his tragic fate to sink beneath the burden of this stolen achievement, which, at the same time, he can by no means cast off. Thus we see the situation prepared in Ibsen's earlier work. It is taken up as it were afresh in *Brand*, where the Mayor seizes on the priest's idea of building the larger church.

The Pretenders is beyond question the work in which Ibsen has attained the greatest degree of perfection. In thus throwing into relief its chief points, we have touched upon only a small number of the extraordinary beauties of this drama. On its faults we will not dwell; they are not difficult to discover, and have been pointed out before.

III

WE have surveyed the series of Ibsen's plays, properly so called, and we have appreciated the striving towards poetic originality which runs through them all, but which attains essential success only in the last. Let us now return to the two lyrical dramas. Why do we not find in them the same originality as in *The Pretenders?* Even if *Love's Comedy* (sometimes to its disadvantage) reminds us of *The Inseparables*,[1] yet the play has in reality no prototype; and no one can deny that *Brand* is a poem which, by the novelty of its whole composition, took the public by surprise, and conquered them at one blow. It is perhaps wiser, however, not to attach too much importance to a conquest like this; it does not necessarily speak in favour of the poem. Every age has its weakness, often an exceedingly grotesque one. That of our day in Denmark is the pietistic and pessimistic moral tendency, which might well take for its motto the not very tasteful lines from *Brand*—

> " Dance, then—but where your dancing ends
> Is quite another thing, my friends."

This tendency appears in good and bad works alike. It rings in our poet's exhortations to an apathetic generation to brace up their muscles; but it is also that which, combined with an element of sensual appeal, sets the stamp of the age on those descriptions which in our day answer to the journeys "through the dens of misery and the abodes of wretchedness." I wonder whether Henrik Ibsen did not feel a little uncomfortable, when *Letters from Hell* seized the opportunity, and sailed forth in the wake of *Brand?* But if the wide acceptance of the book is no proof of its originality, it is at any rate no proof to the contrary. What detracts from the originality in both the polemical poems is simply this, that even if the ideas they express have not previously found

---

[1] A comedy by J. L. Heiberg.

utterance in poetry, they have done so in prose literature.   In other words, these poems do not set forth new thoughts, but translate into metre and rhyme thoughts already expressed. They both stand in *direct* relation to the thinker, who, here in Scandinavia, has had the greatest share in the intellectual education of the younger generation, namely, Sören Kierkegaard. *Love's Comedy*, although its tendency is in the opposite direction, finds its points of departure in what Kierkegaard, in *Either—Or* and *Stages on the Path of Life*, has said for and against marriage. And yet the connection in this case is very much slighter than in the case of *Brand*. Almost every cardinal idea in this poem is to be found in Kierkegaard, and its hero's life has its prototype in his.   It actually seems as if Ibsen had aspired to the honour of being called Kierkegaard's poet.   But he has thereby wronged his genius, taken a lower place than that which he has been called to fill, reduced himself to a sort of collaborator, a position for which he is in reality too great.[1]

Independently of this circumstance, however, both *Brand* and *Love's Comedy* undoubtedly deserve the attention they have aroused. *Brand* led the way.[2] It was a book which left no reader cold.   Every receptive and unblunted mind felt, on closing the book, a penetrating, nay, an overwhelming impression of having stood face to face with a great and indignant genius, before whose piercing glance weakness felt itself compelled to cast down its eyes. What made the impression less definite, namely, the fact that this master-mind was not quite clear and transparent, rendered it, on the other hand, all the more fascinating.

True poetry has the double property of exciting and soothing, of rousing and reconciling; its art consists in voluntarily sacrificing beauty in order to gain in beauty.   It is therefore certain, on the one hand, that a drawing-room poetry which ventures nothing, wins nothing; but it is no less clear that even a glowing rhetoric, which thrills one to the very marrow, and declares war to the death on spiritual apathy, can never be more than one element of poetry.

The poetic art desires war only for the sake of peace; it lets its forces wrestle with one another only to make the final harmony

---

[1] Compare p. 70 of the present work, however. (Author's note in edition of 1898.)
[2] In introducing Ibsen to the Danish public—not in date of composition or publication.

all the more full and deep and elevating. Merely soothing poetry
is in no danger of transgressing the limits of art; it is always
occupied with antiquated ideals. Not so awakening poetry. It
stands in very serious danger of producing so crudely personal,
so disturbing and aggressive an effect, that it may cease to give
the impression of art. There is a very evident movement in this
direction in the poetic literature of Scandinavia. It begins with
Heiberg's *A Soul after Death;* but in this poem the poetic
humour was still light, and the standard æsthetic, not moral.
The next step is Paludan-Müller's *Adam Homo.* Here the
seriousness is far greater, the jesting already much heavier in
its flight. In Henrik Ibsen's *Brand* all jesting has completely
vanished. In Ibsen bitter indignation is the one prevailing force.
Its heavy weapons permit of no distant skirmishing, but press hard
and pitilessly upon the age. The misfortune is not that poetry
here puts on a polemic character; that it already did when, in
Oehlenschläger's time, it defended its own cause against the
prose of a Philistine world. The misfortune is that in our day
poetry fights under the banner of a narrowly interpreted religion,
and often so uncompromisingly and exclusively that it appears
hostile to the whole imaginative life, whose glorified image it is.
Highly characteristic in this respect is Brand's forbidding Agnes
to let her fancy dwell upon the dead child.

But poetry affords no room for this self-contradiction. A
crisis cannot but supervene, in which much poetic genius will be
disintegrated into great, unharmonised talent, and during which
much poetic work will resolve itself into poetic elements which
only in the future our own or the next generation will be able to
master and mould into poetry of a higher order. This general
critical condition has found its especial victim in Ibsen, to whom
an unpropitious destiny seems to have allotted the task of serving
as the representative of polemical poetry, and recording turning-
points in development. And the reason of this is chiefly that
Ibsen, although he has already entered the period of mature
manhood, has not yet taken complete possession of himself as
a poet.

Of this *Brand* gives manifold evidence. The first testimony
is furnished by its external form. One cannot but admire the
ease in versification, and the command of language that is required
to write so long a book from beginning to end in short rhyming

lines (often rhyming trebly and quadruply), whose form admits of
no departure from the once accepted metrical scheme.   But if we
pay closer attention to these rapidly thrown-off lines, we shall
find that it is with them as it is with the verses in *Love's Comedy*.
They have both impetus and vigour; indeed, at their best the
true divine frenzy which, according to the dictum of the ancients,
denotes the poet: but the course lies as much over stocks and
stones as if the Muse's cothurni were the actual red shoes of
Andersen's tale.   We stumble now over an inelegant combination of words, now over an inappropriate simile, now over an
expression that only incompletely clothes the thought; and we
have only this consolation, that we very quickly rise again.   The
broken doggerel Latin in the concluding lines affords an example:—

> "Svar mig Gud, i dödens slug ;—
>   gælder ej et frelsens fnug
>   mandeviljens *qvantum satis*—?
>   En röst
>   Han er *deus caritatis!*" [1]

If we now add to this the fact that the dialogue, which in
some places is sublime in its simplicity, in others (for instance,
in the long colloquies between the Mayor and Brand) is unduly
diffuse, we cannot deny that the flowing diction, which is Ibsen's
strong point, is far from being controlled by a perfect sense of
unity in style and tone.

And as, on the whole, the pen has flown too fast in the poet's
hand, so also his wrath, which in Byronic fashion is turned
especially against his own countrymen, has sometimes run away
with him so as to impair the effect he would otherwise have
obtained.   He has made the characters who are the butts of his
satire represent themselves with such open self-irony that they,

---

[1] Thus rendered by Professor Herford :—
> "God, I plunge into death's night,—
> Shall they wholly miss Thy Light
> Who unto man's utmost might
> Will'd——?
>   *A Voice.*
>   He is the God of Love."

It should be said that the expression "mandeviljens *qvantum satis*" is first used
by the doctor in the third act of *Brand*, so that Brand is here simply quoting it, so to
speak. Dr. Brandes cites with disapproval another couplet from *Brand*, but as it has
disappeared from recent editions it need scarcely be preserved in this place.

so to speak, give themselves one slap in the face after another.
For instance, the Mayor uses the expression: " I am visibly
moved," of himself, and between Einar and Brand in the fifth act
the following words are exchanged :

> " *Einar.* . . . I turned me thence
> To preach for Total Abstinence ;
> But since that Work for the unwary
> Is strewn with perilous temptation,
> I chose another occupation,
> And travel now as Missionary——
> > *Brand.* Where ?
> > *Einar.*   To the Caudate-Nigger State.
> But now I think we'll separate ;
> My time is precious——
> > *Brand.*   Won't you stay ?
> You see here's festival to-day.
> > *Einar.* Thanks, no ; the swarthy Heathens wait.
> Farewell."

By laying on the colour so thickly, the poet robs the figure of
its natural life.   Stupidity and vileness have stirred in him an
indignation too strong and unqualified to be controlled.   It is
the same with the enthusiasm that is the cause of his wrath, the
reverse side of his exasperation.   In the hero of the poem the
enthusiasm could not be too strong or too ardent ; but it ought
not to have infected Ibsen himself to such an extent that he is
wholly and utterly carried away by his hero, whose one-sidedness
it is, after all, his purpose to condemn.   Ibsen has conjured up a
spirit that he himself is powerless to control.   He makes Brand
the mouthpiece for so many thoughts for the truth of which he
himself wishes to vouch, that one receives from his work the
impression that he is crying out to the world : " I feel that in
all this there must be a mistake, but where it really lies I am not
able to make clear either to myself or to others."   For this reason
the last words of the poem carry with them no conviction ; for
Brand has beaten every objection out of the field, and has already
admirably refuted the charge which meets him at the moment of
his death, the charge of not having understood that God is love.
For this reason an attack on Brand transforms itself all too easily
into an attack on the poet, who has not let his protagonist

meet either a hero who was truer, or an irony that was stronger, than himself.   Brand makes the greatest possible claims on others, while he himself is in the very midst of his development.   He preaches the uttermost renunciation as a duty at the same time that he himself is taking a wife.   He not only lacks the cleverness, but also the wisdom, without which one cannot wholly serve the good.   And all this the poet allows to pass because he has allowed himself to be overawed by his hero.   Not even where Brand becomes almost comic, as the hardy Norseman who can neither weep nor feel cold—not even there is irony allowed to seize its opportunity and clear up the misunderstanding.

I am far from suggesting that the poet's own judgment should follow close on the heels of the action like a running commentary all through the play ; but presented as it is at last without any motivation, it sounds like an unjustifiable decision.   The words in which it clothes itself, that God is love, have already been employed by apathetic dulness ; and profound though the observation be that temptation and grace may speak in the selfsame terms, yet little is done to make clear the difference between them. As a poetic idea, then, the fundamental thought lacks justification : the poet has left the reader to form his own unaided opinion as to the one-sidedness of the hero.   Nor does the hero justify himself as a poetic ideal—where the poet has tried to produce the impression that he is in the right, the reader is generally indignant with him.

In æsthetic language, this deficiency is called the absence of motivation.   The lack of motive for an action, the absence of plan, purpose, and object in it, may of course itself be motived by the state of mind of the actor ; and this is partly the case when Brand, in the last act, sets forth into the mountains with the whole parish at his heels ; but far oftener in this poem the deficiency of motive is simply an imperfection.   It applies to the most important as well as to less significant matters ; almost from first to last we feel the lack of adequate motivation.   We are surprised when we come upon anything so deeply and satisfactorily motived as Agnes's application of the words : " Whoso sees Jehovah, dies ;" for Ibsen has not accustomed us to anything of the kind.   Why is Brand, in the first act, in such desperate haste ?   How can he, in the fourth act, hope so much from having the church rebuilt ? These and many similar questions receive no satisfactory answer. So deeply, indeed, is this want of motive rooted in the soul of the poem, that it even, when it takes the form of a lack of purely logical cogency, tempts the intelligence to hypercriticism. Where Brand sacrifices his son, the inhuman dilemma is not so sharply defined but that many ways of evading it could be imagined—for instance, Brand himself might remain, while the child might be sent away to a milder climate. The least poetical reader may here call the poet to account.

What explains this weakness in the composition is the fact that the poem is a poem of ideas. Traits which lack a motive do not necessarily lack a reason. Most of them have their deeper reason—their design—in the requirements of the fundamental idea; and what may in itself seem rather a vague fancy (for instance, the rebuilding of the church), cannot be rightly understood until it is understood symbolically. The symbolism all through is, indeed, deep rather than clear; but several of these symbols give such masterly expression to profound thoughts, that for their sake one is reconciled to much obscurity. Among these I class such traits as Brand's final engulfment in Nature's wild ice-church—a church in which every one is in great danger of ending who turns his back upon such spiritual churches as already exist.

The success of *Brand* among the Danish public led Ibsen to reprint the work which, in 1862, had appeared in Christiania under the alluring but somewhat pretentious title of *Love's Comedy*. The play has an advantage over *The Inseparables* in its larger subject. It is more than a biting, searching satire on modern betrothals and marriages ; it turns upon the nature and significance of love itself; and the conclusion at which it arrives is that love must of necessity be one of two things—either lasting, but a thing of mere habit, or passionate, but like the flame of a moment, either imaginary or hollow, either dead as a log or fugitive as a bubble. This melancholy view of life saturates the play from Falk's first despairing song, which, with the precision of a tuning-fork, strikes the keynote of the whole, up to the bewildering final scene in which the lovers, distrusting the durability of their passion, and its fitness to form the basis of a marriage, separate almost at the very moment when they have found each other. There is about as

much and as little justification here as in *Brand*. The polemical
tendency robs the play of the character of a drama; there is no
action in it, there is declamation; there is no conversation, but
hissing and lashing; there is no fighting with the polished, shining
swords of speech, but with its heavy ordnance, whose volleys are
more noisy than effective. The hero is an Erasmus Montanus [1]
of the first water, and we sadly miss the corporal's staff. These
are true, deep words that his lady-love addresses to him :—

> " I saw in you no falcon,[2] but a kite,
> A poet-kite, a paste-and-paper thing,
> Wingless itself, and impotent for flight,
> While all its virtue centres in its string.
> Thus you lay powerless at my feet and whined :
> ' Oh, set me soaring, one way or another !
> Defy your sister and ignore your mother,
> But help my songs and me to breast the wind ! ' "

In these words lie the possibility and germ of a radical change
in Falk's character, but the possibility is not realised, and the
germ of better things is stifled. Neither the play of intellect and
wit with which the poem sparkles, nor its wealth of ingenious
similes, striking points and catchwords, nor the epigrammatic
terseness of its dialogue, can prevent the reader from standing on
his guard against its breaches of true refinement and healthy
feeling. On the contrary, they only keep him alive to the necessity
for caution.

[1] The hero of one of Holberg's greatest comedies. The " corporal's staff," in
the last Act, drubs him into conformity with the beliefs of his day and his village.

[2] The hero's name, "Falk," means "falcon."

IV

ONE source of most of the imperfections of the later Norwegian
school of poetry is its will to do too much. A definite artistic
effort engrosses the imagination; one is conscious of too much
exertion and purpose. Many great artists have really "willed"
nothing at all; they have written, painted, and composed as
Mozart composed when he wrote *Don Giovanni*. In Ibsen the
supremacy of the will is apparent in the part that reflection plays
in his writings; for with him reflection is the medium through
which the will works upon the imagination. I have often, in the
preceding pages, been compelled to use the word "thought," when
my purpose was to emphasise the poetical element in Ibsen. It
does not speak in a poet's favour when there is a frequent necessity
for employing this word. Poetry always seems to come to him as
material which does not bring with it its form, but for which a
form must be deliberately chosen; his principal figures are in-
carnate ideas, and the sign of deficient inspiration in his works
is always that the figure will not round itself to many-sided
organic nature. We instinctively long for a stereoscope, in order
to see these figures properly. Ibsen's propensity for the abstract
and symbolical is due to this limitation of his talent. In the first
place, it is the origin of the abstract figures in his dramas, which
are merely emblematical personifications of a single quality in
human nature. Already in his first work, *Catilina*, Furia is a
symbol compounded partly of one side of Catiline's own character,
partly of another nature; and Gerd stands in the same relation
to Brand. The fact that Bishop Nicolas in *The Pretenders* is
represented as such an abstract and inhuman incarnation of evil
scarcely arises, as has been supposed, from a desire on the poet's
part to thrill the nerves, but from his inability to resist the inclination to expand the figure from a person to a principle.

In the second place, this limitation of Ibsen's talent introduces
something dry, thin, and schematic into his method of composition.

He finds it difficult to avoid a certain dead symmetry, and sometimes he is imprudent enough himself to reduce his characters to
ideas, thus giving the impression of a dance of death in which the
personages have suddenly lost their flesh and blood, and become
mere naked skeletons. Look, for instance, at the conclusion of
the first act of *Brand* :—

> " Which wildest reel, which blindest grope,
>   Which furthest roam from home and hope :—
>   *Light-heart*, who, crowned with leafage gay,
>   Loves by the dizziest verge to play,—
>   *Faint-heart*, who marches slack and slow,
>   Because old Wont will have it so ;—
>   *Wild-heart* who, borne on lawless wings,
>   Sees fairness in the foulest things?
>   War front and rear, war high and low,
>   With this fell triple-banded foe ! "

How the lovers, the peasant, and Gerd herself dwindle down
at these words into three naked categories !

Lastly, its preponderant reflectiveness gives to Ibsen's
dialogue its striking and powerful, but sententious character.
Speeches such as the following are significant: "Sing? Nay,
nay; yesterday I could sing; I am too old to-day!" (Örnulf in
The Vikings, Act iv.), or, "A man can die for another's life-
work, but if he is to go on living, he must live for his own"
(Skule in *The Pretenders*, Act v.). Ibsen has many such characteristic sentences; but on the other hand he has not infrequently
marred his works by speeches that seem to come from a spectator
rather than an actor. In these the reflectiveness is felt to be
nothing less than a disease. And even where Ibsen does not go
to extremes, as in the Mayor's and Einar's speeches in *Brand*, he
with difficulty avoids letting the characters utter sentences that
are far too general, self-conscious, and suitable to a thousand
occasions, when one would expect them to be exclusively taken
up with what is happening to themselves personally, to them
alone, in this particular situation.

Look at this fragment of dialogue from *The Pretenders* :—

" *King Skule.* Every fair memory from those days have I wasted
and let slip.
" *Ingeborg.* It is man's right to forget.

"*King Skule*. And meantime *you*, Ingeborg, loving, faithful woman, have sat there in the north, guarding and treasuring your memories, in ice-cold loneliness!

"*Ingeborg*. It is woman's happiness to remember."

This, if sententious, is still beautiful; but the poet reveals all too distinctly what he wants us to learn from this meeting when he afterwards makes Ingeborg leave the stage with these words, which she says to herself:—

"*To love, to sacrifice all, and be forgotten, that is woman's saga.*" [1]

Happily, however, there are certain spots in Ibsen's poetic domain into which self-conscious reflection does not enter; he sometimes succeeds in grasping humanity in such living forms, that he satisfies every demand, even the most extreme, for reality and individual life. He is especially successful in his female figures; it almost seems as though woman's character, being more closely allied than man's to the mysterious, maternal element in nature, offers a greater resistance to his disintegrating reflection. Again, he portrays filial affection excellently, perhaps because this too, as something simply and directly natural, wears in his eyes a sort of *noli me tangere* aspect, which he has disregarded only once, in depicting Brand's relation to his mother. He has beautifully embodied filial reverence, with a very few touches, in the youthful figure of Nils Stensson in *Lady Inger of Östraat*. Brought face to face with a mother such as his, Nils suddenly feels himself insignificant and ignorant; the determination to be worthy of her changes him in the twinkling of an eye from a boy to a man. In *The Pretenders*, Peter's reverence for his royal father is depicted with great feeling, as also the beautiful relation between Hakon and Inga, who is so proud of her "great son." And yet it is perhaps possible, both in these pictures of natural affection and in several of Ibsen's delineations of love, to trace the poet's reflection, developed at the expense of feeling. Very frequently when Ibsen depicts love, whether between son and mother, son and father, or two lovers, the love is strongly mingled with admiration. Woman's love, with him, is apt to be love of a man's fame (Eline in *Lady Inger*, Hjördis in *The Vikings*,

---

[1] Ibsen has, in later editions, modified these speeches. Ingeborg now says: "It was your right;" "It was my happiness;" and "To love, to sacrifice all, and be forgotten, that has been my saga."

Ingeborg in *The Pretenders*); but even if admiration is an element in all love, especially in nineteenth century love, and in love as the nineteenth century represents it, and above all in woman's love, yet admiration is precisely head-love rather than heart-love; in real, natural love, untainted by reflection, admiration, as such, has not yet come to the surface at all. Juliet does not admire Romeo. Be this as it may, however, Ibsen has in more than one instance represented the unmixed emotion and passion, in its unfathomable depths and its inscrutably elevated enthusiasm.

Here are a few examples, the first from *Lady Inger of Östraat*. The second scene of Act iii., the conversation between Nils Lykke and Eline, contains, in spite of a few tasteless touches, a delineation of the birth of love in a woman's heart, that is simply admirable in its truth. The young girl hates with all her proud nature the man who stands before her; at any rate she ardently wishes to hate him; but at every speech love rises higher in her heart, fills it and deepens it. The scene ends thus :—

"*Nils Lykke.* We shall meet no more ; for before daybreak I shall be gone. So now I bid you farewell.
"*Elina.* Fare you well, Sir Knight!
  (*A short silence.*)
"*Nils Lykke.* Again you are deep in thought, Elina Gyldenlöve! Is it the fate of your fatherland that weighs upon you still ?
"*Elina* (*shakes her head, absently gazing straight in front of her*). My fatherland ? I think not of my fatherland.
"*Nils Lykke.* Then 'tis the strife and misery of the time that cause you dread.
"*Elina.* The time? I have forgotten time. . . . You go to Denmark? Said you not so ?
"*Nils Lykke.* I go to Denmark.
"*Elina.* Can I look towards Denmark from this hall ? "

Thus does love speak.

An example from *The Pretenders*. Hakon is chosen king. As king, he is forced to part from Kanga, his paramour, and to take a wife. Statecraft bids him choose Margrete, Skule's daughter, who, as it happens, has long loved him secretly. Can anything be more beautiful than these speeches :—

"*Hakon* (*warmly*). Earl Skule, to-day have I taken the kingdom from you; let your daughter share it with me !

" *Earl Skule.* My daughter !

" *Margrete.* Oh God !

" *Hakon.* Margrete, will you be my Queen ?
    (*Margrete is silent.*)

" *Hakon* (*takes her hand*). Answer me.

" *Margrete* (*softly*). I will gladly be your wife.

   .   .   .   .

" *Hakon* (*approaching Margrete*). A wise queen can do great things in the land : I have chosen you fearlessly, for I know you are wise.

" *Margrete.* That only !

" *Hakon.* What mean you ?

" *Margrete.* Nothing, my lord, nothing.

" *Hakon.* And you will bear me no grudge if for my sake you have had to let slip fair hopes.

" *Margrete.* I have let slip no fair hopes for your sake.

" *Hakon.* And you will stand ever near me, and give me good counsel ?

" *Margrete.* I would fain stand near to you.

" *Hakon.* And give me good counsel. Thanks for that ; a woman's counsel profits every man, and henceforth I have none but you—my mother I have sent away——

" *Margrete.* Ay, she was too dear to you——

" *Hakon.* And I am King. . . .

" *Margrete* (*smiles sadly*). Ay, I know 'twill be long ere you send me away.

" *Hakon* (*brightly*). Send you away ? That will I never do !

" *Margrete* (*with tears in her eyes*). No, that Hakon does only to those who are too dear to him."

But beautiful as this picture is, neither it nor any other is so remarkable as the representation in *Brand* of a mother's love for her dead child ; all its mysteries, so impenetrable to the ordinary man, its poetry, its almost frenzied worship, Ibsen has unveiled with a truth that is the more impressive because this poem, in the rest of its design, is so destitute of love. Agnes's poring over the little dead boy's clothes, or even more, the scene in which she places the candle in the window, so that its light may fall across the snow upon his grave, and give the little one a gleam of Christmas comfort, is itself like a bright, shining window whence warmth falls upon the poem's snow-field, or like a clear, sparkling eye that animates a pale and coldly serious countenance. One is tempted to exclaim, " Have you been a woman in some other life, since you thus know a woman's heart ? "

These female figures augur well for Ibsen's future ; they are prophetic of "life's summer-lands," towards which Brand, even in death, so earnestly yearns, and which we heartily trust the poet may reach.   But to this end it will be necessary for him to get clear of the track on which he has entered in writing *Love's Comedy* and *Brand*.

V

THE above was already written when *Peer Gynt* appeared. This book follows all too closely in the footsteps of the two polemical dramas. Its point of departure and the name of its chief character are taken from an old Norwegian folk-story. Among Asbjörnsen's fairy-tales there is a story which may be condensed as follows: In olden days there was a hunter named Peer Gynt, who was continually up in the mountains shooting bear and elk. Once, late in the autumn, he was going to the mountains. All the people had by that time left the upland pastures and gone home, with the exception of three sæter-girls, who were keeping company with the trolls. When he came nearly up to the sæter where he was going to spend the night, it was so dark that he could not see his hand before his face, and the dogs barked so incessantly that it was quite eerie. Suddenly he ran against something, which, when he touched it, was cold and slippery and big; he did not know what it was, but it was certainly uncanny. "Who's that?" he said. "Oh, it's the Boyg," was the answer. Peer Gynt was none the wiser for this; however, he went a little to one side of the hobgoblin, thinking he must be able to get round it. But in vain. He again runs into something, which, when he touches it, is once more big and cold and slippery. The same question, the same answer. Once more he attempts to get round it, and once more he receives this answer to his question, "Oh, it's the great Boyg." Peer shoots and dislodges the hobgoblin with his shot, though without injuring it. The same Peer goes through many a combat with trolls and goblins; he drives away the trolls living with the before-mentioned sæter-girls, he rids a farm on the Dovrefjeld of trolls; and for the rest it is said of him that "Peer Gynt had not his equal as a romancer and story-teller. He always declared that he himself had taken part in the adventures that people said had happened in olden days." Out of these and many other little touches

Ibsen's drama has developed, and one cannot but frequently admire the deep and yet obvious meaning and coherence the poet has managed to give to materials which, in the folk-story itself, have very little meaning, and are combined at random.

The object of *Peer Gynt* is once more to represent the moral nature of mankind from its seamy side.   The hero, like a scape-goat, is laden with every human baseness, only that the general weakness and worthlessness is here mainly represented by a single vice, namely, that of seeking to romance oneself away from life, or life away from oneself, and trying by the aid of fancies to "get round" all serious and vital things, until one's character is hardened and ossified in egoism.   That which is described as a disease in Schack's *Visionaries*, is here condemned as a sin. What Ibsen here wishes to deal a blow at is the disposition so much talked and written about since Goethe's time, to hold real life aloof through the power of imagination—the tendency defined by Kierkegaard as "the natural and sensual man's method of parrying the ethical claim."   Peer Gynt himself is the incarnation of cowardly egoism in the guise of self-deception and falsehood.   Like Adam Homo,[1] he sinks ever lower, and at last only obtains salvation—a very doctrinary trait—through a woman, in whose love, trust, and hope he has always, in spite of all his vileness, existed in his ideal nature.

What great and noble powers are wasted on this thankless material!   Except in the fourth act, which has no connection with what goes before and after, and is witless in its satire, crude in its irony, and in its latter part scarcely comprehensible, there is almost throughout a wealth of poetry and a depth of thought, such as we do not find, perhaps, in any of Ibsen's earlier works.

The first act is a beautiful, vivid, and enthralling exposition, in which the half symbolical, half allegorical marvels with which the book is afterwards burdened are totally absent.   There is a strength of imagination and a real humour in this act which carry one with them, and pique one's curiosity as to what is coming. The second act is weaker, but yet has great lyrical beauties.   The third is wholly beautiful; there is powerful imagination, deep feeling, and a note of mournful romance in the description of Solveig's arrival at the settler's hut, and in the affecting present-ment of the mother's death.   The fifth act has yet another poetic

---

[1] In Paludan-Müller's poem of that name.

pearl of great price in the priest's funeral discourse at the grave
of the poor fellow, Peer Gynt's antithesis, whose horizon was so
narrow, but who did his duty like a man within his allotted sphere;
and this act has every here and there remarkably profound and
beautiful passages, such as the scene in which Peer Gynt peels
the onion, that in which the voices around him remind him of
what he should have done, and others too numerous to mention.
But the allegory has so fatally sapped the power of the poetry,
that even masterly details can scarcely assert themselves in the
midst of all the indistinctness and unintelligibility.

It would be unjust to deny either that the book contains great
beauties, or that it tells us all, and Norwegians in particular,
some important truths; but beauties and truths are of far less
value than beauty and truth in the singular, and Ibsen's poem
is neither beautiful nor true.   Contempt for humanity and self-
hatred make a bad foundation on which to build a poetic work.
What an unlovely and distorting view of life this is! What acrid
pleasure can a poet find in thus sullying human nature?   This
kind of endeavour must one day reach the end of its tether.
Taine has somewhere remarked, in opposition to all such poetical
moralising, "Man is not an abortion or a monster, nor is it the
mission of poetry to revolt or defame men.   Our inborn human
imperfection is part of the order of things, like the constant defor-
mity of the petal in a plant; what we consider a malformation is a
form; what seems to us the subversion of a law is the fulfilment
of a law."

This means that the poet has another mission than that of
libelling human nature, as Ibsen does in the fourth act of this
poem.   It further means that the poet has another mission than
that of being a moralist.   He must, indeed, have his philosophy,
even if it be not philosophically formulated; but his very philosophy will forbid him to moralise.   The moralist is a man who
sets to work with a single ultimate object, moral improvement, in
view, and therefore confines his attention wholly to a single side
of life.   The moralist, for instance, is the man who founds tem-
perance leagues, and who thinks he has won a victory when he
has succeeded in rooting out the one propensity against which he
has declared war.   The philosopher, on the contrary, is the man
who, if he has his attention directed to the injurious effects of
over-indulgence in alcohol, will first consider whether alcohol is

not a necessity for the lower classes, a means of forgetfulness such as we others have in science and art, and whether, if it is abolished, its place will not be taken by other, perhaps much more stupefying and maddening stimulants, experience having taught him that no nation can entirely dispense with such things. Well, as Ibsen himself says in *Peer Gynt*, "Some take to brandy, and others to lies"; the poet who continues so long to stare at falsehood, self-deception, and fantasy, that at last he almost blindly runs amuck against it, is, from the poetic point of view, only a moralist. Were he a philosopher, as a poet ought to be, instead of fighting like a berserk against self-delusion, he would have assigned to fantasy its proper place in the economy of human life, and would have seen that illusion, besides being a dangerous and pernicious power—which will be readily granted—is, to a certain extent, in the first place unavoidable, and therefore necessary, in the second place beneficial, comforting, and beautiful— as, for instance, the illusion that the sky is blue, not black—and therefore in a double sense necessary. But, for the present, Ibsen feels it neither his pleasure nor his duty to take such a view ; he is no longer in his element except as a polemist.

SECOND IMPRESSION

(1882)

SECOND IMPRESSION

(1882)

I

WHEN Henrik Ibsen, at the age of thirty-six, left Norway to go into the exile from which he has not yet returned, it was with a gloomy and bitter mind, after a youth spent on the shady side of life. At the time of his birth, in the little Norwegian town of Skien, his family was in a position of precarious affluence. Both his parents belonged to the most respected families in the town; his father was a merchant in a varied and extensive business, and was fond of showing unlimited hospitality. But in 1836 he failed, and nothing was left for the family except a country property in the vicinity of the town. Thither they removed, and thus dropped out of the circles to which they had previously belonged. In *Peer Gynt*, Ibsen has used the circumstances and recollections of his own childhood as a kind of model in the description of the life in the wealthy John Gynt's household. His home seems to have had no great attraction for him.

Although these conditions mean less in so poor and democratic a country as Norway than they would elsewhere, and although Ibsen does not seem to have lacked either the youth's or the poet's faculty of rising above adverse reality by virtue of enthusiasm for ideas and an independent imaginative life, yet early poverty always sets its mark on the mind. It may breed submissiveness, or it may develop germs of revolt; it may render a man ill at ease, or self-reliant, or hard for his whole life. Upon Ibsen's solitary, combative, and satirical nature, more calculated to impress than to prepossess his surroundings, it must have acted as a sort of challenge. It probably rendered him ill at ease in society, and produced in him some ambition in the direction of

external badges of honour that should place him on an equal foot-
ing with the class with which, as a youth, he did not associate,
together with an overpowering feeling of being completely thrown
upon himself and his own resources.

Ibsen, who, in the course of years, has grown so staid, and
whose days pass with the regularity of clock-work, is said to have
lived a somewhat irregular life as a young man, and was therefore pursued by that ill-repute, which even a trifling irregularity,
especially when it is the irregularity of genius, calls forth in
little places where nothing can pass unseen. I can imagine
Ibsen in his early manhood, worried by creditors, and daily
executed *in effigie* by the moral censorship of tittle-tattling
cliques. He had written no small number of beautiful poems,
and a series of dramas that are now famous, and some of
them among the most admired of his works; but they were
published in Norway, in hideous editions, on bad paper, sold
to the number of a few hundred copies, and earned for the
poet, even on the part of his friends, only a tolerably frigid
acknowledgment of his talent. He grew tired of Norway.
In 1862, following the polemical and sarcastic bent of his
nature, he had published *Love's Comedy*, which united a cutting
scorn for Philistine erotics, with a profound distrust of the sustaining power of love through the changes of a lifetime, and
strong doubt of its ability to retain its ideality and enthusiasm
unimpaired and unchanged through wedded life. It could not be
unknown to the poet that society, with all the insistence begotten
of the instinct of self-preservation, had made confidence in the
unchangeableness of normal and healthy love an obligatory article
of faith ; but he was young and defiant enough to give a qualified
sanction to the most commonplace conception of marriage in the
union of Guldstad and Svanhild, rather than refrain from ex-
pressing his doubts as to the orthodox conception of love. The
book evoked a howl of exasperation. People were furious at
this attack on the amatory institutions of society—engagements,
marriages, and so forth. Instead of taking it to themselves, they
began, as is customary in such cases, to search into Ibsen's
private life, and investigate the nature of his own marriage. As
Ibsen once put it to me : the printed criticism of the comedy
might have been borne at a pinch, but the oral and private
criticism was absolutely intolerable. Henrik Ibsen was con-

demned as a talented *mauvais sujet*. Even a work of such excellence as *The Pretenders*, which followed in 1864, failed to rehabilitate the poet's name. It was not, I believe, quite inappreciatively judged by the critics, but neither was it estimated at its proper worth, and it made no stir. I do not think twenty copies of it came to Denmark ; at any rate it was *Brand* that first made the poet's name known out of Norway. The foregoing essay, of 1867, was the first connected account ever published of his career as a poet. To Henrik Ibsen's private grounds for despondency was added a feeling of profound dissatisfaction with Norway's political attitude during the Dano-German war. In 1864, in spite of the promises given at the great assemblies of students, and reiterated by the Scandinavian party in the press—pledges which Ibsen had regarded as obligatory —Norway and Sweden declined to assist Denmark against Prussia and Austria. For all these reasons, his native country, which seemed to him the abode of pettiness, apathy, and faint-heartedness, became so hateful to him, that he turned his back upon it.

Since then he has lived by turns in Italy, in Dresden, in Munich, in Italy again, and again in Munich—passing from five to seven years at a time in each of the German towns. But he has had no permanent abode. He has led a quiet, regular, family life ; or rather, within the setting of a family life, he has found his real life in his work. He has associated in public places with the leading men of his places of sojourn, and has received numbers of migratory Scandinavians in his house ; but he has lived as in a tent, among pieces of hired furniture, which could be sent back on the day appointed for his departure. Since 1864, he has not had his feet under his own mahogany, nor slept in his own bed. He has never, in the stricter sense of the word, settled down ; he has accustomed himself to feel at home in homelessness. When I last visited him, on my asking whether nothing at all in the flat he occupied belonged to him, he pointed to a row of pictures on the wall: they were the only things that were his own. Even now, when he is a wealthy man, he feels no longing to possess a house and home, and still less a farm and lands, like Björnson. He is separated from his people ; he has no work that connects him with any institution or party—not even with a magazine or newspaper—at home or abroad. He is a solitary man. And in his isolation he writes :—

> " My countrymen, who poured in draughts unsparing
>   The wholesome, bitter tonic-drink wherethrough,
>   Though sick to death, I nerved myself anew
> To face the fight of life with steadfast daring—
>   My countrymen, I send you greeting !—you,
> Who lent me Fear's wing'd sandals for my faring,
> Who lent me Exile's staff and Sorrow's pack—
> Lo! from afar I send you greeting back."

He sent many and weighty greetings. But all his productions, both before and during his exile, bear one and the same stamp, the stamp of his natural disposition, unrestrained and grim. This fundamental mood, so natural in the homeless, comes to the surface whenever Ibsen is most effective. Let us call to mind a few of his most peculiar, and indeed most dissimilar productions. Think of the poem *On the Uplands*, in which the speaker, from high up on the mountains, sees his mother's cottage burning, with her inside, while he himself, will-less and despairing, sits noting the picturesque effect of the flames amid the moonlight; think of *Home Life*, where the poet's creatures of fancy, his winged children, take flight as soon as he sees himself in the mirror with blue-grey eyes, close-buttoned jacket, and felt slippers; think of the grimly thrilling poetry of the scene where Brand wrests from his wife the clothes of their dead child; think of the passage where Brand lets his mother go to hell, and that scene, so admirable in its profound originality, where Peer Gynt lies his mother into heaven; think of the poem, *A Corpse in the Cargo*, or of the painfully intense impression produced by *A Doll's House*, where we see a butterfly who, through three acts, is pricked with a needle, at last transfixed by it—if we think of all these things, we perceive that the fundamental mood, answering to a painter's landscape back-ground, is, in all the pathetic parts, an intense grimness. It may rise to terror, to tragedy, but it is not primarily due to the fact that the poet is a tragedian. Schiller's and Oehlenschläger's tragedies are only occasionally grim, and even the writer of *King Lear* and *Macbeth* has written harmoniously tender things, like *A Midsummer Night's Dream* or *The Tempest*. But with Ibsen the mood of grimness is always the underlying one. It would naturally arise in a born idealist, who from the very first thirsted for beauty in its highest forms—ideal, intellectual beauty—and in a born rigorist, who, being thoroughly Germanic and peculiarly Norwegian in disposition and temperament, and subject, moreover, to the religious influences of his surroundings, was inclined to regard the life of the senses as ugly or sinful, and seriously to admire or acknowledge no beauty save moral beauty. At bottom he was shy, that is to say, so constituted that it did not require many disappointments to make him shrink into himself, with his heart full of distrust of the world around him. How early he must have been wounded, repulsed, humbled, as it were, in his original inclination to believe and to admire! His first deep impression as an intellectual individuality must, I imagine, have been the impression of the rarity—or non-existence as he probably put it in bitter moments—of moral worth ; and disappointed in his search for beauty, he doubtless found a sort of solace in unveiling everywhere the sad truth that lies behind appearances. The air around him resounded with words that expressed ideals ; they spoke of everlasting love, deep earnestness, the courage of faith, firmness of character, Norwegianness :—

> " And stormy cheer and song go round
> For the small Folk, rock-will'd, rock-bound."

He looked about him, he searched, he probed, and found nothing in the world of reality that answered to these words. Then there grew out of this very longing for the ideal a peculiar power in him of seeing hollowness everywhere. It became an instinct with him to test whatever seemed genuine, and without much astonishment convince himself of its falseness. It became a passion with him to tap with his finger on everything that looked like metal, and a kind of painful satisfaction to him to hear the hollow ring which at the same time wounded his ear and confirmed his suspicion. Wherever he encountered so-called greatness, it became a habit and a necessity for him to ask, as in the *Rhymed Letter to a Swedish Lady :* "Is the great then really great ?" He had a keen eye for the egoism and untruth which may underlie the imaginative life, for the bungling which the phrases of political freedom and progress may cover ; and as time went on a superb

ideal (or moral) *suspiciousness* became his muse.   It inspired him
to ever bolder investigations.   Nothing awed or frightened him,
neither what looked like idyllic happiness in family life, nor what
passed for dogmatic certainty in social life.   And the bolder the
investigations became, the greater dauntlessness did he acquire
in communicating, announcing, proclaiming the result.   It became
his chief intellectual delight to disturb, to provoke, all whose
interest it was to cloak abuses in extenuating euphemisms.

Just as it had always seemed to him that there was far too
much talk about ideals which were never to be met with in life,
so did he feel with ever more indignant certainty that, as if by
common consent, men were silent as to the deepest, most incur-
able failures of their ideals, as to the real, actual horrors of life.
In good society they were passed over as improbable or unmen-
tionable, in poetry, as unpleasant; for æsthetic theory had banished
from polite literature whatever was too trenchant, whatever
was unmistakably and immitigably painful.   Thus did it happen
that Ibsen became the poet of the grim side of life, and hence his
inclination to vindicate his own position against the multitude, in
bitter and cutting phrases.

Henrik Ibsen's personal appearance is suggestive of the
qualities he has revealed in his poetry.   The severe or sarcastic
expression of his face conceals a delicate spirituality that only occasionally breaks through.   Ibsen is short and thick-set; he dresses
with a certain style and elegance, and looks very distinguished.
His walk is slow, his carriage dignified and stately.   His head is
large and striking, with its thick mane of greyish hair, which he
wears rather long.   The forehead, which dominates the face, is
remarkable; abrupt, high, broad, and yet perfectly formed, it
bears the stamp of greatness and spiritual wealth.   The mouth,
when in repose, is compressed, as if lipless; closed and resolute,
it reveals the fact that Ibsen is a man of few words.   And he
does often sit silent in general company, like the taciturn, sometimes almost gruff doorkeeper of his mind's sanctuary.   He can
talk *tête-à-tête*, or in quite a small circle, but even then he is anything but communicative.   I once in Rome showed Runeberg's
bust of him to a Frenchman, who remarked : " The expression
is more spiritual than poetic."   One can see in Ibsen's face that
he is a satirist and thinker, not an enthusiast.   Yet his best short
poems, *Gone*, and a few others, show that at one time or other

during the battle of life, a lyric Pegasus must have been killed under him.

I know two expressions in his face. The first is that in which a smile, Ibsen's kind, beautiful smile, breaks through and animates the mask of his countenance, all the geniality and cordiality that lie deepest down in his heart coming out to meet one. Ibsen is slightly embarrassed in manner, as melancholy, serious natures are apt to be. But he has this charming smile, and smile, glance, and hand-clasp say much that he neither would nor could clothe in words. Sometimes, too, in the course of a conversation, with a sly laugh (*schmunzelnd*, as the Germans say), and an expression of good-natured roguishness, he will let fall some short, sharp, anything but amiable expression of dissent, which nevertheless reveals all that is most amiable in his character. The smile atones for the sharpness.

But I also know another expression in his face, that which is called forth by impatience, wrath, righteous indignation, biting scorn : an expression of almost cruel severity, which recalls the lines in his beautiful old poem of *Terje Vigen* :—

> " But when, on days of storm, his eye
>   Gleamed like the stormy day,
> The boldest came not willingly
>   In Terje Vigen's way."

It is with this expression that, as a poet, he has most frequently shown himself to the world.

Ibsen is a born polemist, and his first poetic utterance (*Catilina*) was his first declaration of war. From the time he came to years of discretion, which in his case was not early, he has never really doubted that if he, the individual, were weighed in the scales with what goes by the name of society (to Ibsen the collective embodiment of those who are afraid of the truth, and who attempt to plaster over sores with phrases) he would certainly not be found wanting. He maintains, among other whimsical paradoxes, that only a certain amount of intelligence is available for distribution at any given time, and that if one or two individuals, as, for instance, Goethe and Schiller in the Germany of their day, are very liberally endowed, their contemporaries will be proportionately stupid. He inclines, I should imagine, to the

opinion that he received his gifts at a time when there were very
few to share in the sum total.

Hence Ibsen does not feel himself to be the son of a fatherland, part of a whole, the leader of a group, a member of a community; he simply feels himself to be a gifted individual, and
the one thing he really believes in and respects is personality.
In this detachment from all natural solidarity, in this vindication
of the spiritual ego, there is something that vividly recalls the
period of Scandinavian history in which he was brought up.
Kierkegaard's influence is the most noticeable.   But Ibsen's
isolation is of a totally different stamp.   Björnson's diametri-
cally opposite disposition has probably contributed not a little
to its development   It always influences a character to be
set by fate in direct contrast with a markedly dissimilar contemporary.   Not unfrequently it is a misfortune to a great man
to see his name constantly coupled with another's, always in comparison, whether for praise or blame.   The compulsory, inevitable twinship is apt to irritate and injure him.   In this case it
may have led Ibsen to exaggerate the marked characteristics of
his temperament, namely, its intensity and reserve.

No one who, like Ibsen, believes in the rights and power of
the emancipated individual, no one who has felt himself, as early
as he did, at war with the world around him, has a favourable
opinion of the multitude.   It is evident that contempt for mankind
developed itself in Ibsen in his early manhood.   Not that he
began by cherishing an exaggerated opinion of his own talent
or his own worth.   His is the seeking, doubting, questioning
nature :

> " To ask is my vocation, not to answer,"

and such minds have no bias towards vanity.   One sees, too,
how long he is in finding his own language and form.   Think of
the crude manner in which he begins with *Catilina;* of the strong
influence of Oehlenschläger on his little unpublished drama, *The
Hero's Grave;* of the way in which *The Feast at Solhaug* recalls,
even in the very metre, a writer so unlike the author as Henrik
Hertz (especially in the latter's drama, *Svend Dyring's House*);
remember the free use he makes in *The Vikings at Helgeland* of
effective traits from Icelandic Sagas, before he ventures to trust
to his own inventive power and his own markedly characteristic

style.[1] It is much nearer the truth to say that Ibsen was one of those natures who set out in life with much humility, ready to recognise superiority in others, until the day of trial brings with it a consciousness of their own power. From that moment, however, such natures are, as a rule, far more stiff-necked than those who were originally self-satisfied. They weigh, as on an invisible balance, those whose superiority they formerly acknowledged, and, finding them too light, they throw them on one side.

In Ibsen's eyes the average man is small, egoistical, and pitiful. He looks upon him, not from the purely scientific, but from the moral point of view ; and in his character of moralist, he dwells far more on the badness of man than on his blindness and foolishness. In Flaubert's eyes, man is bad because he is stupid ; in Ibsen's, he is stupid because he is bad. Think, for instance, of Thorvald Helmer. He all along judges his wife stupidly, stupidly as an ass. When Nora is saying a last farewell to Dr. Rank, when the man prepared to meet death is face to face with the woman resolved to seek it, and is answering her with compassionate tenderness, Helmer stands by with outstretched arms, the personification of intoxicated sensual desire. But his stupidity arises solely from his self-righteous egoism.

Ibsen considers mankind to be pitiably bad, not actively wicked. I was long ago struck by an aphorism in Kierkegaard's *Either—Or*, which seems very appropriate as a motto for Ibsen : "Let others complain of this age as being wicked, I complain of it as being contemptible, for it is devoid of passion. Men's thoughts are thin and frail as lace, they themselves are the weakling lace-makers. The thoughts of their hearts are too paltry to be sinful." What but this does Brand say, when he complains of the God of his generation, and contrasts him with his own God, his own ideal ?

> "Ye need, such feebleness to brook,
> A God who'll through his fingers look,
> Who, like yourselves, is hoary grown,
> And keeps a cap for his bald crown.
> Mine is another kind of God !

---

[1] Later remark. In the preface to the second edition of *The Feast at Solhaug*, published in 1883, twenty-seven years after the first, Ibsen has protested against the theory of his having been influenced by Henrik Hertz.—G. B.

Mine is a storm where thine's a lull,
Implacable where thine's a clod,
All-loving there, where thine is dull ;
And he is young like Hercules,
No hoary sipper of life's lees ! "

What does the Button-Moulder say but this ? He answers
Peer Gynt in much the same way as Mephistopheles in Heiberg's
A Soul after Death answered " the Soul." Peer Gynt's destina-
tion is not the lake of fire and brimstone ; far from it ; he is only
to go into the casting-ladle and be melted down again ; he was
no sinner, for " it needs both strength and earnestness to sin " ;
he was simply second-rate :

"So into the waste-box you needs must go,
    And then, as they phrase it, be merged in the mass."

Peer Gynt, in Ibsen's mind, is the typical expression of the
national vices of the Norwegian people. They inspire him, as we
see, less with horror than with contempt.

This view of the matter explains even those of Ibsen's youthful works in which the author's originality is still undeveloped.
Though such a character, for instance, as Margit in *The Feast at
Solhaug*, inevitably recalled Hertz's Ragnhild to Danish readers,
yet it is a character of quite different stuff from Hertz's—harder,
fiercer, and more resolute. A woman of the present day who
loved madly and hopelessly would feel herself more akin to
Ragnhild than to Margit ; Margit is an intimation to such a
woman that she, the reader, is the child of a degenerate age,
devoid of the courage and consistency of passion, miserable in her
half-heartedness. And why does Ibsen in *The Vikings* go back
to the wild tragedy and magnificent horror of the Völsung myth ?
In order to offer such a picture to the present age, to awe, to
shame this generation by showing it the greatness of its fore-
fathers—the passion that swiftly and ruthlessly presses towards
its aim, the proud strength that disdains words, that acts silently,
suffers silently, dies silently ; wills of iron, hearts of gold ; deeds
which a thousand years have not sunk in oblivion. Look at
yourselves in the mirror !

Take the first expression of this militant fervour, *Catilina*,
a drama conceived with all an undergraduate's enthusiastic

sympathy. Catiline despises and hates Roman society, where violence and self-seeking reign, where a man becomes ruler by intrigue and cunning; and he, the individual, rises in rebellion against society. Take the same militant fervour in one of Ibsen's latest works, that admirable drama, *A Doll's House*—there it comes subdued, but no less cutting, from a woman's lips. When Nora, the little lark, the squirrel, the child, finally braces herself up and says, " I must find out who is right, society or I,"—when this frail creature dares to place herself on the one side and the whole of society on the other, we feel that she is Ibsen's daughter. Then take the same habit of mind in its last expression, so alarming to many. When Mrs. Alving says, speaking of the conventional dogmas of society: " I wanted only to pick at a single knot; but when I had got that undone, the whole thing ravelled out. And then I understood that it was all machine-sewn "—one hears through the words, in spite of all the distance separating the poet from the created character, his sigh of relief at having once, even if indirectly, made a clean breast of it.

Catiline and Mrs. Alving, Ibsen's earliest and latest characters, convey the same sense of isolation as the intervening creations, Falk, Brand, and Nora; there is in all the same desperate running of the head against a stone wall.

The accepted name in modern Europe for such a view of the world and mankind is pessimism. But pessimism is of many kinds and shades. It may, as in the case of Schopenhauer and Von Hartmann, consist in the conviction that life itself is an evil, and that the sum-total of happiness in a human life is infinitesimal in comparison with its sum of pain and suffering; it may demonstrate the worthlessness of all we value most — prove the sadness of youth, the joylessness of labour, the emptiness of pleasure, and our utter indifference to it when it becomes a thing of custom. The holders of these views will either, like Schopenhauer, prescribe asceticism, or, like Von Hartmann, recommend labour in the cause of progress, even while realising that every advance in civilisation brings with it an increase of human misery. This is not Ibsen's pessimism. He too finds the world bad, but he does not concern himself with the question whether life is or is not a blessing. He looks on things entirely from the moral point of view.

The pessimistic philosopher dwells on the illusory nature of love, shows how little happiness it brings, and how that happiness is practically illusion, the aim and object of love not being the felicity of the individual, but the greatest possible perfection of the coming generation. To Ibsen, love's comedy does not consist in the inevitable erotic illusion—in that alone he sees no comedy; that has his full sympathy—but, in the degeneration of character attendant on the prosaic Philistinism of the usual legal union, originally contracted with erotic motives. The metamorphosis of the missionary enthusiast, on his engagement, into a teacher in a girls' school—that is a subject for *his* satire, that is love's comedy for him. Only once, as it were in a flash, has he risen high above his usual moral standpoint in regard to erotic conditions, and that is in *Complications*, not only the wittiest, but also the most profound of all Ibsen's short poems; though even here he still writes as a satirist.

The pessimistic philosopher dwells with predilection on the thought of the unattainableness of happiness, alike for the individual and for the race. He lays stress on the thought that pleasure slips away between our fingers, that all we desire comes to us too late, and that what we do attain is far from having that effect on our minds, which the desire for it had conjured up before us. He sees in an utterance like Goethe's famous remark that in seventy-five years he had not had four weeks' actual pleasure, but had been continually trying to turn over a stone which always fell back into its place again, a decisive proof of the impossibility of happiness. For how can that which Goethe, the favourite of gods and men, did not attain, be attained by common every-day mortals ! Not so Ibsen. Sceptical as he is, he does not actually doubt the possibility of happiness. Even Mrs. Alving, who has been so sorely wronged by circumstances, believes that under other conditions she might have been happy, believes that her wretched husband himself might have been happy. And Ibsen is evidently of her opinion. What she says about the "half-grown town" that has "no joys to offer, only dissipations, no object in life, only an official position, no real work, only business," comes from Ibsen's heart. Life itself is not an evil. Existence itself is not joyless. No, some one is to blame, or rather many are to blame, when a life is lost to the joy of life ; and Norwegian society, depressing, coarse in its pleasures, enslaved to conventional ideas of duty, is pointed out as the culprit.

To the pessimistic philosopher, optimism is a kind of material-
ism.   He fears that optimism, preached as he hears it in every
street, threatens a world-catastrophe.   According to him, what is
wanted is to teach the masses that they have nothing to hope
from the future; the pessimistic creed of universal suffering is the
only one that can make the futility of their efforts clear to them.
This view is never found in Ibsen.   When he touches a social
sore, as in *The Pillars of Society*, and elsewhere, it is always one
of a moral nature.   Some one is to blame for it.   Whole strata of
society are rotten, whole rows of society's pillars are decayed and
hollow.   The close air of the small community is unhealthy; in
wide spheres there is room for great actions.   A breath from without, that is to say, a breath of the spirit of truth and liberty, has
power to purify the atmosphere.

Hence Ibsen, looking on the world as bad, feels no compassion
for men, only indignation.   His pessimism is not of a metaphysical, but of a moral nature, and is based on a conviction of
the possibility of realising ideals; it is, in a word, the pessimism
of indignation.   And his want of sympathy with many kinds of
suffering results from his conviction of the educative power of
suffering.   Only through suffering can these small, miserable men
become great.   Only through struggle, defeat, and chastisement,
can these small, miserable communities become healthy.   Ibsen,
who himself has felt the bracing power of adversity, who has
drained the wholesome draught of bitter experience, believes
in the utility of pain, of adversity, and of oppression.   This is
perhaps most evident in his *Emperor and Galilean.*

Ibsen's acquaintance with historical documents concerning
Julian and with Julian's own writings, is evidently considerable.
And yet there is little of the historical in his general conception
of the character.   He has robbed the man of his real greatness.
He has seen him, not indeed as he appears to the orthodox
churchman, but still with Christian eyes.   He lays stress on a
persecution of the Christians with which the real Julian would
have nothing whatever to do.   His conception of Julian is, that
by this persecution of his Christian subjects, he became the real
creator of the Christianity of his age, that is to say, its awakener
from the dead.   To Ibsen, Julian's significance in world-his-
tory is this : By transforming Christianity from a court and
state religion into a persecuted and oppressed faith, he restored

to it its pristine spiritual impress, and its primitive passion for martyrdom. Defied by the Christians, the emperor punishes with severity, but his punishments have an effect never dreamt of by him. His old fellow-students, Gregory, who had not the courage for any decisive action, but had "his little circle, his family to guard," and had neither power nor ability for more, and Basilios, who devoted himself to "poring over the writings of worldly sages on his country estate," even these now arise, strengthened by persecution, like lions in his path.

II

IT is plain that an author does not put the whole of himself into his books. Indeed, his personality sometimes produces quite a different impression from that conveyed by his writings. This is not the case with Henrik Ibsen. And I am in a position, after an acquaintance of many years, to cite a number of small traits which show that he does not hold the opinions above set forth for the sake of attracting attention or of selling his books.

With the help of a few unconsidered utterances, which, whether jest, paradox, or metaphor, throw light on the poet's inner life (but which, though stored up in a good memory, cannot of course lay claim to perfect accuracy), and also with the help of a few written expressions of opinion, to the publication of which he has given his consent, let me attempt to give a more vivid and correct impression of the principal traits of Ibsen's mind than could be derived from his books alone.

When France in 1870 lay mutilated and bleeding at the feet of Germany, Ibsen, whose sympathies at that time were mainly with France, was far from sharing in the feeling of depression produced in the Scandinavian countries by the issue of the war. While all other friends of France were profuse in their expressions of sympathy, Ibsen wrote (20th Dec. 1870):—

"My thoughts are much occupied by the great events of the day. The old, illusory France has collapsed; and as soon as the new, real Prussia does the same, we shall be with one bound in a new age. How ideas will then come tumbling about our ears! And it is high time they did. Up till now we have been living on nothing but the crumbs from the table of last century's revolution, a food out of which all nutriment has long been chewed. Our terms stand in need of a new connotation, a new interpretation. Liberty, equality, and fraternity are no longer the things they were in the days of the late lamented guillotine. This is what politicians will not understand, and therefore I hate them. What they want is special revolutions, revolutions in externals, in the political sphere. But all this is mere trifling. What is really wanted is a revolution of the spirit of man."

No one can fail to see in this letter the historical optimism to which I have already drawn attention. In spite of the despondency attributed to him, Ibsen has the firmest hope, the strongest confidence in the new life that will arise out of social convulsions; nay, is even persuaded that only so long as those convulsions which accompany the birth of ideas into the world keep men's minds on the alert, are the ideas themselves a living power. The very guillotine has so little terror for him that the sound of its falling knife chimes in harmoniously with his optimistic and revolutionary theories. It is not liberty as a dead condition that seems of value to him, but liberty as an aspiration, a struggle. Lessing declared that if God held out truth to him in his right hand and in his left the pursuit of truth, he would seize the left. Ibsen would subscribe to this declaration, if the word "liberty" were substituted for "truth." His detestation of politicians is due to the fact that in his opinion they conceive of and treat liberty as something external, soulless.

Ibsen's optimistic and, so to speak, didactic conception of suffering is strikingly illustrated by his eager desire that Norway should aid Denmark in her struggle for Schleswig. His arguments were of course those of Scandinavians generally—the kinship of the two nations, the promises which had passed between them, Denmark's rightful cause—but it was his optimism that led him to regard as of secondary importance the question whether the assistance of Norway would have been of any avail. To the exclamation, "You would have got a sound thrashing!" he retorted, "Of course; but what would that have mattered? It would have brought us into the movement, into touch with Europe. Anything rather than remain mere outsiders!"

On another occasion, I think it was in 1874, Ibsen was loud in his praises of Russia. "A splendid country!" he said with a smile; "think of all the grand oppression they have!"

"How do you mean?"

"Only think of all the glorious love of liberty it engenders. Russia is one of the few countries in the world where men still love liberty and make sacrifices for it. That is why she holds so high a place in poetry and art. Remember that they own a writer like Turgueneff; and they have Turgueneffs among their painters too, only we don't know them; but I have seen their pictures in Vienna."

"If all these good things come of oppression," I said, "we are bound to praise it. But the knout—are you an admirer of that too? Suppose you were a Russian, should your little boy there," pointing to his half-grown son, "have the knout?" Ibsen sat silent for a moment, with an inscrutable expression, and then answered, laughing, "He shouldn't get the knout; he should give it." The whole of Ibsen is in this humorous subterfuge. In his dramas he is continually giving his generation the knout. Doubtless his hope was that the knout in Russia would eventually, by way of variety, fall on the oppressors.

One cannot wonder that, holding such views, Henrik Ibsen was anything but delighted when Rome was occupied by the Italian troops. He wrote in whimsical despondency :—

" . . . And so they have taken Rome from us human beings, and given it to the politicians! Where shall we take refuge now? Rome was the one sanctuary in Europe, the one place that enjoyed true liberty — freedom from the political liberty-tyranny. . . . And then the delicious longing for liberty—that is now a thing of the past. I for one am bound to confess that the only thing about liberty that I love is the fight for it; I care nothing about the possession of it. . . ."

There seem to me to be two sides to this political attitude. On the one side we have a reminiscence of romanticism, in that abhorrence of the rule of utility common to the romantic schools of every country; on the other, we have the personally characteristic belief in the power of the individual, and predilection for propounding radical dilemmas. He who in *Brand* formulated the watchword, "All or nothing!" can lend no willing ear to the practical politician's cry: "One step forward every day." I wonder whether one of the causes of the above-mentioned partiality for Russia might not be found in the fact that in that country there is no parliament. Ibsen's whole character presupposes a distrust and ill-will towards parliamentarism. He believes in the individual, in the single great personality; the individual, and he alone, can accomplish everything. Such a body as a parliament is in Ibsen's eyes a mere assembly of orators and dilettanti; which of course does not imply that he can feel no respect for a member of parliament simply as an individual.

Hence it is a never-failing source of amusement to Ibsen to read in the newspaper: "A commission was then appointed," or, "Thereupon an association was formed." He sees a sign of the degeneracy of the day in the way in which every one who takes up a cause or plans a scheme promptly tries to get a commission appointed or to found a society for its advancement. Think, for instance, of the scornful laughter that rings through *The League of Youth*.

I believe that in his own private mind Ibsen pushes his individualism to an extreme of which his works give no adequate idea. On this point he resembles Sören Kierkegaard, except that he goes even farther than Kierkegaard went. He is, for instance, an extreme opponent of the sharply defined modern idea of the State. Not that he approves of small states or small societies. No one can entertain a greater horror of the tyranny they exercise, and the narrow-mindedness they beget. Hence few have expressed themselves more warmly than he in favour of the Scandinavian kingdoms following the example of Italy and Germany, and uniting themselves into one political whole. His greatest historical drama, *The Pretenders*, treats of and vindicates such an amalgamation-idea. On this point Ibsen goes so far, that he seems to overlook the dangers to the multiplicity and variety of intellectual life which must accompany the striving after political unity. Italy never attained greater artistic eminence, and never stood higher generally, than when Siena and Florence were two worlds; and Germany never occupied a higher intellectual and general position than when Königsberg (Kant) and Weimar (Schiller, Goethe) were important centres. But in spite of his enthusiasm for unity, Ibsen's poet's brain dreams of a time when the State shall concede a far greater measure of individual and municipal liberty than it does now, and when, consequently, states as we now understand them shall no longer exist.

Although Ibsen reads extremely little, and does not take any special trouble to make acquaintance with his own times by means of books, he has often seemed to me to stand in a sort of mysterious correspondence with the fermenting, germinating ideas of the day. Once or twice I have even had a distinct impression that new ideas, which were on the point of manifesting themselves publicly, but were not yet perceived by others, had been occupying and as it were tormenting him. Immediately after the conclusion of the great Franco-German war, at a time when all minds were taken up with it, and when the possibility of anything like the Commune in Paris had scarcely suggested itself to a single Scandinavian mind, Ibsen put before me, as political ideals, conditions and principles the exact nature of which I do not clearly recollect, but which were undoubtedly closely akin to those publicly proclaimed by the Paris Commune, in a much distorted form, exactly a month later. Referring to the difference in our views on liberty and politics, Ibsen wrote to me (February 17, 1871):—

"The struggle for liberty is nothing but the constant active appropriation of the idea of liberty. He who possesses liberty otherwise than as an aspiration possesses it soulless, dead. One of the qualities of liberty is that, as long as it is being striven after, it goes on expanding. Therefore, the man who stands still in the midst of the struggle and says, 'I have it,' merely shows by so doing that he has just lost it. Now this very contentedness in the possession of a dead liberty is characteristic of the so-called State, and, as I have said, it is not a good characteristic. No doubt the franchise, self-taxation, &c., are benefits—but to whom? To the citizen, not to the individual. Now, reason does not imperatively demand that the individual should be a citizen. Far from it. The State is the curse of the individual. With what is Prussia's political strength bought? With the absorption of the individual in the political and geographical idea. The waiter is the best soldier. And on the other hand, take the Jewish people, the aristocracy of the human race—how is it they have kept their place apart, their poetical halo, amid surroundings of coarse cruelty? By having no State to burden them. Had they remained in Palestine, they would long ago have lost their individuality in the process of their State's construction, like all other nations. Away with the State! I will take part in that revolution. Undermine the whole conception of a State, declare free choice and spiritual kinship to be the only all-important conditions of any union, and you will have the commencement of a liberty that is worth something. Changes in forms of government are pettifogging affairs—a degree less or a degree more, mere foolishness. The State has its root in time, and will ripe and rot in time. Greater things than it will fall—religion, for example. Neither moral conceptions nor art-forms have an eternity before them. How much are we really in duty bound to pin our faith to? Who will guarantee me that on Jupiter two and two do not make five? . . ."

Henrik Ibsen certainly cannot have been acquainted with the anonymous "Barrister's" no less ingenious than paradoxical attempt to show in what way two and two may be imagined to make five on Jupiter; nor is it probable that he had any idea how loudly Stuart Mill and other adherents of radical empiricism would have applauded the last-quoted line; it is the natural bent of his mind that has led him to this all-embracing scepticism, which in him is so remarkably combined with vigorous faith. Did not his Brand say :—

> "It is not for a Church I cry,
> It is not dogmas I defend;
> Day dawn'd on both, and, possibly,
> Night may on both of them descend.
> What's made has 'finis' for its brand;
> Of moth and worm it feels the flaw;
> And then, by nature and by law,
> Is for an embryo thrust aside."

The letter above quoted forms a vigorous commentary on these words, and affords, moreover, a proof of Ibsen's inspired apprehension of what is going on under the surface of the age. The following extract may be given without danger of lowering him in public estimation, since even Prince Bismarck has publicly acknowledged that there lurked a "grain of sound sense" at the heart of the Commune's ill-fated endeavours. On 18th May 1871, Ibsen wrote :—

". . . Is it not villainous of the Commune in Paris to have gone and spoilt my excellent state-theory, or rather non-state-theory? The idea is ruined for many a day; I cannot in decency even proclaim it in verse. Yet it has a sound kernel, that I see clearly; and some day it will be put into practice without any caricature. . . ."

It is his persistent exaltation of the individual that places Ibsen in an attitude of antagonism towards the accepted theories of the State and of society. I am not sure that I quite understand him on this point; his train of thought is alien to me. I understand how men like Lorenz von Stein and Gneist see in modern history one constant feud between the State and society, and how they, with a new and invigorating conception of the State idea, turn against society; I can also understand how a new conception of society

may lead to abhorrence of the State; but I cannot quite understand the ambiguity of Ibsen's attitude, and do not even know
whether Ibsen himself is conscious of any ambiguity in it.

He carries even further his anxiety lest the sting of personality
should be blunted and its best part sacrificed.   He believes that, in
order to develop all the fruitful possibilities of his nature, the
individual must first and foremost stand free, stand alone; and
he therefore has a watchful eye for the dangers in this respect
that every association, even friendship, even marriage, brings
with it.   I remember his answer to a letter written by me in one
of those desponding moods to which young people give such free
expression, in which I had told him with a little sigh that I had
few or no friends.   Ibsen wrote (6th March 1870):—

". . . You say that you have no friends at home.   That is what I
have fancied for a long time.   When a man stands, as you do, in a
close personal relation to his life-work, he cannot really expect to keep
his friends. . . . Friends are a costly luxury, and when one invests
one's capital in a vocation or a mission in life, one cannot afford to
have friends.   The expensiveness of friendship does not lie in what
one does for one's friends, but in what one, out of regard for them,
leaves undone.   This means the crushing of many an intellectual germ.
It is an experience that I have gone through, and consequently I have
to look back on a number of years during which it was not possible for
me to be myself. . . ."

Is not all Ibsen's independence of character and loneliness of
spirit felt in these ironic words, "the expensiveness of friendship"?   And does not the whole passage give some explanation of
the comparatively late development of his originality?   As I have
already asserted, it is evident that Ibsen began his career with
no excessive amount of self-confidence.

And as with friendship, so with marriage; it too, under certain
circumstances, may be a hindrance to the independence of the
individual.   Therefore it is that Nora refuses to consider her
duty towards her husband and her children the most sacred of
all; there is a duty more sacred still—her duty towards herself.
Therefore it is that she answers Helmer's "Before all else, you
are wife and a mother," with, "I believe that before all else I am
a human being—or at least that I should try to become one."

Ibsen shares with Kierkegaard the conviction that in every

human being there slumbers a mighty soul, an unconquerable
power; but he differs from Kierkegaard in holding this essence
of individuality to be human, while Kierkegaard looks upon it
as something supernatural.   According to Ibsen, a man is to
develop his individuality, not for the sake of higher powers, but
for his own sake.   And as the first condition of this development
is that he shall stand free, and be his whole self, concessions to the
world are to him the principle of evil, the great enemy.   Here we
arrive at the fundamental idea of *Brand*.   Remember how Brand
says :

> " But from these scraps and from these shreds,
> These headless hands and handless heads,
> These torso-stumps of soul and thought,
> A man complete and whole shall grow,
> And God His glorious child shall know,
> His heir, the Adam that He wrought ! "

Hence the necessity for such an apparently inhuman motto as
" All or nothing."   Hence it is that the " spirit of compromise,"
even in the hour of death, appears to Brand only as the temptress
who would have his little finger in order that she may possess
herself of his whole hand.   And we have the same spirit of compromise reappearing in *Peer Gynt* in the form of the Boyg, the
embodiment of all that is cowardly and yielding in man, all that
turns aside and goes round about :—

> " Strike back at me, can't you ! "
>   " The Boyg isn't mad."
> " Strike ! "
>   " The Boyg strikes not."
>   " Fight !   You shall ! "
> " The great Boyg conquers but does not fight."
> .   .   .   .
> " The great Boyg conquers in all things by yielding."

To wrest humanity from the suffocating embrace of the Boyg,
to take captive the spirit of compromise, bind it hand and foot
and cast it into the depths of the sea, this has been the aim of
Ibsen, the poet.   And this wresting of the individual from the
power of compromise and of the Boyg is the revolution as he
conceives it.

I once asked Henrik Ibsen: "Is there one among all the Danish poets whom you, at your present stage of development (1871) care at all about?" After letting me guess for some time in vain, he answered: "Once upon a time, somewhere in Zealand, there walked behind his plough an old man in a smock-frock, who had looked upon men and things till he was wroth at heart; that is a man I like." Is it not significant that Bredahl should be the Danish poet who is really most sympathetic to Ibsen? Bredahl, too, was a man whose indignation darkened his outlook on the world, not indeed a very profound psychologist, but a poet in whose loud onslaught on "Stormskjoldbulder"[1] we have, as it were, the thunder preceding Ibsen's lightning. Bredahl sees only the tyranny and hypocrisy that are external and gross, Ibsen searches out the tyranny and hypocrisy that lie hidden in the depths of the heart. Bredahl is still only like the "Revolutionary Orator" of Ibsen's poem: he "provides the deluge," while his great successor, going more thoroughly to work, "has pleasure in placing a torpedo under the ark."

I have called Ibsen a revolutionary nature. I need hardly protest against being misunderstood to mean by this that his is a nature which enthusiastically welcomes outward, violent changes. Far from it; the very reverse is the case. Solitary as he is and feels himself to be, unfavourably disposed towards all parties, simply as parties, refined, polished, reserved, "awaiting the approach of the time in a spotless wedding-garment," he is, in a purely external sense, rather to be classed as a conservative—a strange kind of conservative indeed—conservative out of radicalism, because he expects nothing from piecemeal reforms. At heart he is a determined revolutionist, but the revolution for which he longs and works is the purely spiritual one of which I have already spoken. The reader will not have forgotten the concluding words of that letter of December 1870, quoted above: "What is really wanted is a revolution of the spirit of man." They are words I can never forget; for they in a manner represent Ibsen's whole poetical "programme"—an admirable "programme" for a poet to put forth.

[1] Christian Hviid Bredahl (1784–1860) is called by Dr. Brandes (*Mennesker og Verker*, p. 32), "the coarse and wild dramatist of indignation - pessimism." "Stormskjoldbulder" (literally "Storm - shield - rumble") is one of the leading characters in his *Dramatic Scenes Extracted from an Antique Manuscript*, a series of fantastico-satirical dramas or dialogues.

I should, however, be false to my own convictions if I were to say that Ibsen's philosophy of life seems to me to contain more than a strong element of truth. It is a philosophy of life in virtue of which a man may think and may write poetry, but he cannot act; nay, in the present state of society, he is hardly even justified in speaking out plainly, because he thereby in a manner calls on others to act, which in this case is equivalent to rushing on their ruin. He who, from the height of his aspiration after great, decisive, sweeping revolutions, looks down indifferently or contemptuously on the slow, petty changes of ordinary progress, on the politician's gradual, dilatory, small improvements, on the compromises to which the practical reformer must consent in order to attain even the partial realisation of his idea, and on those associations without the help of which it is impossible for any but an autocrat to carry a single scheme into practical execution—the man, I say, who looks with contempt on all these things, must give up all thought of moving a finger in practical matters. Like Sören Kierkegaard and like Brand, he can do nothing but point to the yawning chasm that separates existing from ideal conditions. If such a man were to take, or induce others to take, active measures to realise his aspirations, he would simply lead his followers headlong over the brink of the dizzy abyss that separates the actual from the desired state of things, and—run the risk of being promptly arrested. Even the poet can only express such extremely ideal views indirectly, suggestively, ambiguously, through the mouths of independent dramatic characters who relieve the author of all responsibility. Only vulgar adversaries could take the grim jest about the torpedo under the ark to be literal, bloodthirsty earnest.

Such a philosophy entails a separation of the theoretical from the practical, of the individual from the citizen, of intellectual liberty from that practical liberty which means responsibility—a dualism which can be carried into practice only by a dramatic poet living in exile, who need have nothing whatever to do with state, society, politics, parties, or reforms.

Nor does the ideal of spiritual nobility inherent in this philosophy seem to me a very high one. It is quite true that a great author best maintains his personal dignity by never being seen in the thick of the fray; it is true that it gives an impression of distinction to hold back, never to interfere in the disputes of the

day, never to write a newspaper article.   But it seems to me
that there is more distinction still in the action of the legitimist
generals who enlisted as common soldiers in Condé's army, and
fought on foot in the foremost ranks.   By so doing they lost not
a whit of their inner, essential dignity.

E

III

We have now arrived at a stage in our examination of the spiritual life of the individual at which we can view it in the light of the literary self-consciousness and aspirations of his age. I expressly say of his age and not of his country, for Ibsen's spirit is as pronouncedly European as Björnson's, in spite of his cosmopolitan culture, is national. The poet's attitude towards the self-consciousness of his age means his relation to its ideas and forms. Every age has its own ideas, which in art disclose themselves in the subject chosen, the ideal striven after.

Ideas are not begotten by the poet. They reveal themselves to the thinker, the student, at his work; they come in the shape of inspired apprehension of some natural law or relation, develop themselves and acquire form in the process of scientific experiment, of historic or philosophic research—grow, and are purified and strengthened in the struggle for existence, until, like the angels of the Bible, they become thrones and principalities and powers, spread their pinions and rule the age.

The poet does not beget ideas; that is not his calling, not his affair. But the true poet is impressed by them while they are yet growing and struggling, and in the idea-battle of his age he takes his place on the side of the ideas. He is carried away by them and cannot help himself; he understands without necessarily having learned. The bad poet, he who possesses nothing of the poet but a mechanical aptitude, inherited or acquired, has no ear for the low rumble that tells of ideas undermining the ground; no ear for the throb of their pinions in the air. Heine, in the preface to his *New Poems*, says that while he was writing them, he seemed to hear the whirring of the wings of a bird above his head. " When I told my friends, the young Berlin poets, about it," he continues, "they looked at one another with a curious expression, and assured me unanimously that such a thing had never happened to them." The whirr which the Berlin poets had never heard, was the wing-winnowing of new ideas.

No poet, however, can write entirely without ideas. The bad
poets too have theirs ; they have those of the past; they give
weak, dull expression to the ideas which the artists of an earlier
period rendered with true poetic fervour. The ideas of their age
as a rule seem to them utterly "unpoetical." They hold it impossible to make poetry out of them.

But he who in his youth (in *The Pretenders*) wrote the me-
morable words, "For you 'tis impossible, for you can but work
out the old saga afresh ; but for me 'tis as easy as for the falcon
to cleave the clouds," has never allowed himself to be long dismayed by the thoughts of his age. To many a new thought he
has given flesh and blood, and by embodying it has propagated
it ; many another he has deepened by pouring into it the wealth
of his feeling. We gain some idea of the urgent necessity he has
felt for standing in a living relation to nascent ideas from the
beautiful lines in which the Balls of Wool reproach Peer Gynt :—

> "We are thoughts,
> Thou shouldst have thought us.
>
> .   .   .   .   .
>
> We should have soared up
> Like clangorous voices,
> And here we must trundle
> As grey-yarn thread-balls.
>
> We are a watchword,
> Thou shouldst have proclaimed us.
>
> .   .   .   .   .
>
> We are deeds,
> Thou shouldst have achieved us !
> Doubt, the throttler,
> Has crippled and riven us."

These are accusing words with which one can fancy the poet
spurring himself on in moments of languor, but which it is impossible to imagine as addressed to himself by Peer Gynt. Can one
conceive the miserable Peer setting himself a watchword ? Can
one reproach him with not having done so ?

Let us now see what subjects and ideals specially engross the
mind of this age. They seem to me to fall naturally into the
following groups :—

1. Those connected with religion (that is, men's reverence

for ideas which they conceive as powers), and with the struggle between those who believe these powers to be natural and those who believe them to be supernatural;

2. Those treating of the contrast between the past and the future, between age and youth, between things old and new, and specially of the contrast and struggle between two successive generations;

3. Those that treat of the various classes of society and their life-struggle, of differences of station, and specially of the contrast between rich and poor, social influence and social impotence;

4. Those treating of the contrast between the two sexes, of the mutual erotic and social relations of men and women, and specially of woman's economic, moral, and intellectual emancipation.

We see religious subjects and problems treated in a great variety of ways in our day, although always in the modern spirit. Let us look at the chief of these varieties. In the greatest poet of the older generation in France, Victor Hugo, a weak species of pantheistic deism asserts itself, in spite of his enthusiastic rationalism; we still trace in him the influence of the preceding century; religion is glorified at the expense of religions; love, which unites, at the expense of dogma, which separates and scatters. By the leading authors of the younger generation, Flaubert, for example, religion is depicted with scientific frigidity, but always from its shady side; to him and his kindred spirits it is a hallucination, which has somehow gained credence. The greatest English poet of our day, Swinburne, is an impassioned poetic heathen, who regards Christianity, to him the denial of nature, as his natural enemy. Italy's greatest modern poet, Leopardi, found rest in a lofty and profound pessimism, leading up to stoic renunciation. Carducci, her foremost living poet, is just as modern and more combative. Germany's chief writers, Gottfried Keller, Paul Heyse, Fr. Spielhagen, and others, have championed a godless but soulful religion of humanity.

In Scandinavia the situation was a peculiar one. The Danish writers of the preceding period had as a rule done homage to orthodoxy. The only philosophic spirit among them, J. L. Heiberg, who at first expressed rationalistic opinions, ended by, apparently at any rate, making concessions to dogma; and the

one serious attempt made in Denmark to undermine the authority
of the Church, Kierkegaard's violent attack on the Establishment,
was not directed against the truth of its doctrines, but exclusively
against the lives of its members, and especially of its clergy, as
not being in accordance with these doctrines. This position of
Kierkegaard's has, until quite lately, determined that of most
Danish-Norwegian literary men. Modern fiction in Denmark
and Norway has seldom or never touched upon the objective side
of the matter, the essence of religion; it has confined itself almost
exclusively to the subjective side, which explains the extraordinary
wealth of clerical characters in this literature, both before and
after the author's emancipation from orthodoxy. The pastors in
Björnson's and Fru Thoresen's peasant-stories indicate the standpoint *before*, those in Björnson's, Schandorph's, Kielland's, and
Ibsen's later works, the standpoint *after* emancipation.

Ibsen follows in Kierkegaard's footsteps. Brought up like
the rest of his generation in the north, under the influence of
romanticism, his attitude towards religion is at first uncertain,
confused. In his own nature there was a double bias, certain to
give rise to inward conflict—an inborn tendency to mysticism,
and an equally strong natural tendency towards hard, dry ration-
ality. In few other men does one find such almost morbid flights
of fancy alternating with such quiet acceptance of the prose of
life. *Brand* and *The Pillars of Society* are as different in one
important point as if they had been written by different authors.
One is pure and simple mysticism, the other pure and simple
prose: the idea of the one is strained to the uttermost, the other
conveys a good homely moral.

No one with any understanding of Norwegian intellectual life
can doubt that the great effect produced by *Brand*, the work
which laid the foundation of Ibsen's fame as a poet, was due to
its being interpreted as a kind of poetic sermon, a Jeremiad, a
work of edification. It was not the real merit of the poem that
impressed the general public, and was the cause of the numerous
editions; no, people flocked to the booksellers to buy *Brand* as
they flock to a church after the appointment of a new and
more energetic pastor. In a correspondence I had with Ibsen
on the subject of this work, he himself expressly asserted
that Brand's priestly calling was a purely external, accidental
detail.

In a letter of the 26th June 1869, he writes :—

". . . Brand has been misinterpreted, at any rate as regards my intention. . . . The misinterpretation evidently has its root in the accident that Brand is a clergyman, and that the problem is expressed in religious terms.   A sculptor or a politician would have suited my syllogism quite as well as a priest.   It would have given the same relief to the feeling that impelled me to write, if, instead of Brand, I had taken, say Galileo, with one modification : he would, of course, have had to remain firm, and not admit that the earth stood still.   Nay, who knows but that my choice, if I had been born a hundred years later, might have fallen on yourself, and your attack on Rasmus Nielsen's philosophy of compromise ?   Upon the whole, there is more objectivity in *Brand* than people have as yet discovered, and on this, as a poet, I pride myself. . . ."

Although I have carefully kept everything personal out of my quotations, I allow myself to publish this jesting reference to the literary controversies of the day, because it shows how little importance Ibsen attached to the clerical element in *Brand*.   A further proof of this is afforded by the following passage from a letter I received from him at the time when the introduction to my book, *Main Currents in the Literature of the Nineteenth Century*, was weighing heavily on my mind :—

" It seems to me that you are now passing through much the same crisis that I passed through when I was about to write *Brand*, and I am sure that you too will be able to find the medicine that will drive the disease out of your body.   Vigorous produ ction is a capital specific. . . ."

It is plain enough that the poet himself lays stress in *Brand*, not on doctrine, but on power of self-sacrifice and strength of character.   Yet, although Ibsen is undoubtedly the best, the only authoritative judge of the intention of his own work, he nevertheless, in my opinion, undervalues the strength of the unconscious influence which led him to choose this subject and no other. This unconscious influence was, it seems to me, the national romantic inclination towards mysticism.   Even reading *Brand* according to Ibsen's own interpretation, the parallelism with Norwegian religious phenomena is no less obvious.   To Danes it could not but seem as if Ibsen had had Kierkegaard in mind, for he too laid the greatest stress on fervour and strength of character. But this misapprehension arose from our having no acquaintance with Ibsen's Norwegian models. From what the poet himself once gave me to understand, I conclude that some such Norwegian dissenting pastor as Lammers had more lot and part in the production of the character of Brand than any directly Danish influence. It must not be forgotten, however, that it was Kierkegaard's agitation that gave the stimulus to Lammers's course of action.

In *Emperor and Galilean*, the Kierkegaard influence, though still strong, is on the wane. The martyr spirit is indeed affirmed to be the criterion of truth, the spiritual lesson of the drama being that only that doctrine which finds willing martyrs among its followers possesses any intrinsic value. But along with this we have a half mystical, half modern determinism, we have a Schopenhauerish belief in the unconscious and irresistible universal will, and lastly, we have the quite modern prophecy that to heathenism and Christianity will succeed a Third Kingdom, in which both will be merged. It is significant of Ibsen's mental attitude that in both his treatments of religious subjects struggle and strife are made much more prominent, and are dealt with far more felicitously, than reconciliation and harmony. "The Third Kingdom" in *Emperor and Galilean* stands as indistinctly in the background as does the concluding "Deus caritatis" of *Brand*.

Ibsen's mind has also been occupied by a class of subject which has received abundant and varied treatment in the modern literature of Russia, Germany, Denmark, and Norway, the subject whose interest lies in the relation to each other of two successive periods or generations, or simply of two ages of human life. During his first period he treated such a subject in *The Pretenders*, during the transition stage between the first and second period, in *The League of Youth*. Both these dramas are fine works, but in neither of them is the strong point historic insight or historic impartiality.

The Pretenders is not a historic drama, properly so called. It has not been the poet's design to give us, in a series of pictures of the past, a representation of human nature as it manifested itself under certain conditions at a certain period. He does not look upon his subject from the historical standpoint, he merely uses history as a pretext. The background of the play is mediæval,

the foreground modern, for Earl Skule is a modern figure. The
historical view would have led the poet to depict Skule as a
thoroughbred aristocrat, and Bishop Nicolas as a fanatical, but
staunch and honest ecclesiastic; for Skule's struggle with Hakon
represents, historically, the aristocracy's last unsuccessful attempt
to restrict the royal power ; and the Bishop's struggle represents
the hatred (justifiable from the ecclesiastical standpoint) of Sverre,
the usurper, the enemy of the Church, and all his race. Instead
of this, Ibsen has made of Nicolas a monster, symbolical of envy,
hatred of the light, the discord and division existing in Norway
from time immemorial; of Skule, an ambitious man, who is
tormented while pursuing the highest aims by an unhappy doubt
of his calling and right to do so. Skule and Hakon stand opposed
to each other as the representatives of two ages, the age of
division and the age of union. But, the poet's interest in psychology being so much stronger than his interest in history, this
contrast is forced completely into the background by the contrast
between the individual characters with their different moral stand-
points. Hakon represents the "king's thought" he has conceived,
and by which he is completely engrossed; Skule does not represent any older historical idea, but only introspective self-distrust.
He steals Hakon's "king's thought" that the possession of it may
give him a right to the throne. He does so in vain; the skald
declares to him that one man cannot live for another's life-work,
a truth which he himself acknowledges. The skald's thought is
not expressed quite clearly, for it should surely be possible for
one man to live for another man's ideas, to appropriate them, and
make them his own flesh and blood, without stealing them and
giving himself out as their inventor. The theft of another's ideas,
not the living for them, would make a man unhappy; and it is
this, as a matter of fact, that causes Skule's unhappiness. It
is Ibsen's nature, however, to be much more interested in the
struggles that go on in the mind of an individual, than in the
struggles between historical powers. What attracted him to
Skule, and made Skule the chief character in the play, is the
interest attaching to his complex nature, his bold, restless spirit,
which even in wrongdoing outshines Hakon's simplicity and confidence of victory—the desperate strength of this great Nureddin,
who, in spite of his desire for Aladdin's lamp, in spite of his theft
of the lamp, is doomed to go to ruin. That disproportion between

power and desire, between will and capability, already depicted in Catiline and in Gunnar in *The Vikings*, reappears here in Skule's position towards Hakon's thought. Skule stands face to face with the "king's thought," as Julian stood face to face with Christianity, overwhelmed by a suspicion of the greatness of the force he is opposing, and in a hopelessly false relation to the grand victorious idea. The psychological interest entirely swamps the historical.

The relation between two successive generations is also dealt with in *The League of Youth*, a drama which very wittily parodies the aspirations of a younger generation, without at the same time showing their justification. No parallel can be drawn between this play and such works as Turgueneff's *Fathers and Sons*, or *Virgin Soil*, which, while severe to the younger generation and merciless to the elder, are nevertheless full of sympathy for both. Ibsen's pessimism has suppressed all sympathy. The only worthy representative of the younger generation in his play is Fjeldbo, a perfectly passive nature. It is scarcely an accidental circumstance that he is a doctor. The able physician plays the *beau rôle* in modern fiction ; he is clearly the hero of the hour. The reason probably is that he can be made use of to personify the ideals of the age : to personify on the theoretic side the scientific spirit, concerned with the conflict between truth and falsehood, and on the practical side humanitarianism, concerned with the conflict between happiness and suffering—the conflicts, psychological and social, which occupy the modern mind.

In Schiller's plays, as well as in those of "young Germany," the struggle for political and intellectual freedom plays a leading part. Contrasts in station, too, are a favourite theme in a considerable number of German plays of an early period, although neither dramatists nor poets generally deal with what we at the present day call the social problem. We catch a glimpse of this problem much earlier in French plays, from the days of Beaumarchais down to Victor Hugo, the question having come prominently before the public at a far earlier period in France than in Germany. In the imaginative literature of our day the social questions of the age have gradually ousted the political from the foremost place. Modern poetry is inspired in many countries by sympathy with the humble ; it reminds those in a higher position of their duties. The question is not one of those that have greatly occupied Ibsen, as a poet, yet he has not infrequently touched upon it. When he wrote *Catilina*, he was too undeveloped to have a right understanding of social questions; but many years after, in *The Pillars of Society*, he aimed a blow at the leading classes in his country. As every one is aware, the play had no social-political tendency whatever; but so deep is its pessimism, that if one were unacquainted with the general position of matters in Norway, and with the poet's attitude towards his public and the parties of the day, one might read such a tendency into it. When it was acted in Berlin, many of the spectators (and those, as I can vouch, not among the least intelligent) fell into the error of supposing that it was written by a socialist. I had repeatedly to explain that the play was the work of the favourite poet (at that time) of the Conservative party in Norway. *The Pillars of Society*, which is in some ways like a continuation of *The League of Youth*, resembles it in bringing out only one side of the subject treated. Here, as almost everywhere else, Ibsen produces his effect by onesidedness.

The subject of the relations between woman and man has always been one of the deepest interest to Ibsen, and has called forth some of his most original, most strikingly modern, expressions of feeling.

In his earliest works these relations receive comparatively traditional treatment. The theme of *The Feast at Solhaug* is that treated later by Björnson in *Cripple Hulda*—the position of a young man between a woman older than himself, whom he has loved as a youth, and the young girl he now wishes to make his bride—a theme of general human interest, but far from a novel one. Then, in both *Catilina* and *Lady Inger*, he takes the somewhat far-fetched but striking subject of the punishment of a man with a dissolute past through his love for a young girl, who returns his love, but at the same time loathes and curses him as the seducer and murderer of her sister.

It is in *Love's Comedy* that he, for the first time, takes as his theme the erotic conditions existing in his own country. It is clear that he was strongly influenced by contemporary Norwegian literature. While Björnson, in his first period, was influenced by national legend and song, Ibsen was set in vibration by the most advanced spirits of his time. Part of the inspiration of *Love's Comedy* may be traced to Fru Collett's novel, *The Sheriff's*

Daughters. This daring book, which created a great sensation in Norway, made, wittily enough, though in less polished form, the same attack on engagements and marriages that we find in Ibsen's bolder, more masculine work. In his similes and figures the direct influence of Fru Collett may be traced. The famous tea-simile in Ibsen's play originates with her. In *The Sheriff's Daughters* we read apropos of love :—

" Protect then, O humanity, this first flower of our life. . . . Watch over its growth and fruitage. . . . Do not lightly disturb its first delicate shoots, in the belief that the coarse leaves which follow are good enough. . . . No, they are not good enough. There is as great a difference between them as between the tea which we ordinary mortals content ourselves with and call tea, and that which the Emperor of the Celestial Empire alone drinks, and which is the true tea; it is gathered first, and is so delicate that it must be picked with gloved hands, after the pickers have washed themselves, I think, forty times."

In Ibsen we have : —

"Dear ladies, each and all of you possess
A small ' Celestial Empire ' of your own ;
There thousands of such tender shoots have blown
Behind the Chinese wall of bashfulness,"

and the passage ends :—

" Therefore the common aftergrowth of trade
Is to the first as sackcloth to brocade ;
In handfuls, husk and stalk and all, they pluck it.
That's our coarse black tea—
Vended by the bucket."

Ibsen has only developed the simile, and given it the more enduring form of verse.

As is well known, the only thing that is indubitable about *Love's Comedy* is its satiric intention. The play contains a satire upon marriage, and yet inspires as little sympathy with the assailants as with the defenders of the existing state of things. It is impossible to tell whether it is the poet's final judgment that in these matters tradition should be adhered to or thrown to the winds. The one thing certain is that he takes a misanthropic view of the engagements and marriages he sees around him. I remember a conversation with Ibsen on the subject of this play, which turned into a discussion on love as it exists between engaged couples in general. I said: "There are diseased potatoes and there are sound potatoes." Ibsen answered: "I am afraid none of the sound potatoes have come under my observation."

We discern nevertheless throughout Ibsen's works an ever-increasing faith in and glorification of woman. It sometimes appears in a jarringly conventional form: for instance in *Peer Gynt*, where (according to the tradition of Goethe's *Faust* and Paludan-Müller's *Adam Homo*) Solveig, by her faithful love, saves the really all-too-unworthy soul of her beloved. But this faith in woman, with which Ibsen seems, as it were, to atone for the contempt in which he holds man, is always present, and has produced a series of beautiful and lifelike female portraits, such as Margrete in *The Pretenders*, drawn in imperishable beauty with a few strokes, and Selma in *The League of Youth*, who is the first sketch of Nora. I remarked in a first criticism of *The League of Youth* that this character of Selma had not sufficient scope, and that Ibsen ought to write an entirely new play for it. This he did in *A Doll's House*.

In my opinion, the modern idea of the emancipation of woman was far from being a cherished and familiar one to Henrik Ibsen at the commencement of his career. On the contrary, he had originally very little sympathy with woman. Some authors have a great deal of the woman in their natures, and may almost be called feminine in temperament. Ibsen is not one of these. He has, I should imagine, more pleasure in talking to men than to women, and he has certainly spent far less of his time in the society of women than poets generally do. Moreover, the modern books which advocate the justice of a change in woman's social position at first found anything but an enthusiastic reader in him. If I remember rightly, he disliked John Stuart Mill's book on the woman question, and Mill's personality as a writer inspired him with no sympathy. Mill's assertion or confession that he owed much, and that the best, in his writings to his wife, seemed especially ridiculous to Ibsen, with his marked individualism. "Fancy!" he said, smiling, "if you had to read Hegel or Krause

with the thought that you did not know for certain whether it was
Mr. or Mrs. Hegel, Mr. or Mrs. Krause you had before you!"

I do not believe that this was a personal aversion unconnected
with his feeling on the subject of the woman's rights agitation.
I believe that Ibsen originally had an antipathy to this whole
movement, attributable either to his education or to natural irrita-
tion at some of the ridiculous forms the movement assumed—an
antipathy destined, however, to give way to a sympathy all the
more enthusiastic. In this case Ibsen's reasoning faculty wrought
the change in his feelings. Like a true poet, he is ready to
be the enthusiastic champion of an idea which at first failed to
interest him, as soon as it is borne in upon him that this idea is
one of the great rallying-points in the battle of progress. And
when, in the last scene of *A Doll's House*, we read those words
that fall like sword-strokes, Helmer's—

"No man sacrifices his honour even for one he loves,"

and Nora's—

"Millions of women have done so,"

words which reveal the gulf that yawns between the husband and
wife, sitting one on each side of the table—yawns more horribly
than the mouth of hell in the old romantic dramas — we feel
not only that Ibsen has saturated himself with the thoughts of
the age, but that in passing through his artist's mind these
thoughts have gained a power and intensity sufficient to drive
them home even into hardened hearts. The play made a powerful and somewhat alarming impression. For centuries society,
through the mouths of its priests and poets, had proclaimed
marriage, based upon love and disturbed by no third person, to
be a haven of bliss. Now this haven was seen to be full of rocks
and shallows—and it was as though Ibsen had extinguished the
beacon-lights.

Ghosts followed. Here again, as in *A Doll's House*, a marriage is investigated, this time one of a totally different character.
What was specially fine and delicate in *A Doll's House* was that
Ibsen had granted so much to the husband. What had he not
conceded to him! The man is thoroughly honourable, scrupu-
lously upright, thrifty, careful of his position in the eyes of strangers and inferiors, a faithful husband, a strict and loving father,

kind-hearted, cultured, &c., &c., *and yet!*—this man's wife is a victim, and his marriage a whited sepulchre.

The man in the marriage into which we gain a deep insight in *Ghosts* is of a very different type—coarse, drunken, recklessly dissolute, but with so much of that power of winning hearts by apparent good-nature, which licentious men often possess, as to make it just possible for his wife to conceal his mode of life and save appearances. By remaining with him, by devoting herself to him, she has not only sacrificed her own well-being and happiness, but has become the mother of a being doomed from his birth, of a son who, on entering manhood, falls a helpless victim to mortal exhaustion, despair, insanity, and idiocy; *and yet!*—that part of society that is represented by Pastor Manders considers that her sacrifice of herself and her son was duty, and that any attempt to rebel against such horrors is crime.

This is the tragedy of the play, and this tragedy dismayed Philistia the Great even more than *A Doll's House* had done. This time it was as if Ibsen had extinguished the stars. "Not a ray of light!"

In *Ghosts* the relations between man and woman are placed in a new light, being, as it were, gauged by the relation of both to the child. The drama is a poetic treatment of the question of heredity. It represents, on the basis of that determinism which is at present the last word of modern science in the matter, the general determination by the parents of the physical and mental nature of the child, and gives this fact an emotional and suggestive background by representing it in connection with the more universally acknowledged fact referred to in the title, namely, the preservation by heredity of feelings (and through them of dogmas), whose original life-conditions have died out and given place to others with which those feelings are at variance.

The choice of subject here is of great interest as throwing light on Ibsen's spiritual development. Here for the first time we see him break through the circle which his individualism is apt to draw round the individual as such. In a letter of 1871 he wrote to me these deeply significant words :—

" . . . I have really never had any strong sense of solidarity, it has simply been to me a traditional dogma—and if one had the courage to leave it wholly and entirely out of consideration, perhaps one might get rid of the ballast which weighs heaviest on one's personality. . . ."

Now, ten years later, his eyes are opened to the meaning of solidarity; he has become thoroughly aware of the fact that no amount of "courage" can enable us to disregard it, but that we all, by the destiny of our birth, are bound up with persons, environed by conditions, that we cannot control. It is evident that Ibsen has, in the course of these years, been coming into ever closer contact with the fundamental ideas of the age.

Thus we see him who, like nearly all the older living writers, at first stood waist-deep in the romantic period, work himself out of it and up from it, by degrees become more and more modern, and at last the most modern of the modern. This, I am convinced, is his imperishable glory, and will give lasting life to his works. For the modern is not the ephemeral, but the flame of life itself, the vital spark, the soul of an age.

The disapproval which *Ghosts* awakened in many circles, and the vulgar criticism of which it was made the object, will certainly not restrain Ibsen's productive instinct, but at the moment it discouraged him. He wrote on this subject:—

". . . When I think how slow and heavy and dull the general intelligence is at home, when I notice the low standard by which everything is judged, a deep despondency comes over me, and it often seems to me that I might just as well end my literary activity at once. They really do not need poetry at home; they get along so well with the *Parliamentary News* and the *Lutheran Weekly*. And then they have their party papers. I have not the gifts that go to make a good citizen, nor yet the gift of orthodoxy; and what I possess no gift for I keep out of. Liberty is the first and highest condition for me. At home they do not trouble much about liberty, but only about liberties, a few more or a few less, according to the standpoint of their party. I feel, too, most painfully affected by the crudity, the plebeian element in all our public discussion. The very praiseworthy attempt to make of our people a democratic community, has inadvertently gone a good way towards making us a plebeian community. Distinction of soul seems to be on the decline at home. . . ."

The storm raised by *Ghosts* could have no other effect on Ibsen than that of strengthening him in his conviction of the foolishness of the great majority. He wrote on this subject to me (3rd January 1882):—

" Björnson says: ' The majority is always right;' and as a practical politician he is bound, I suppose, to say so. I, on the contrary, must of necessity say, 'The minority is always right.' Naturally I am not thinking of that minority of stagnationists who are left behind by the great middle party, which with us is called Liberal; but I mean that minority which leads the van, and pushes on to points which the majority has not yet reached."[1]

What augurs well for Ibsen's future work is the fact that in proportion as he has become more modern he has become a greater artist. The ideas of the new age have not with him assumed the form of symbols, but of persons. In earlier years he had a partiality for great symbolic figures, such as Brand, Peer Gynt, &c.; but strange to say, the more thoughts he has conceived, the clearer have they become, and the more artistically has he represented them. His technical mastery has increased in later years from work to work. In *A Doll's House* he surpassed the technique of the most famous French dramatists, and in *Ghosts* (in spite of the unsatisfactory episode of the fire at the asylum) he displayed a dramatic certainty, simplicity, and delicacy which recalled antique tragedy in the hands of Sophocles (Œdipus Rex).

This steady advance is due to the serious view which Ibsen takes of art, and to his conscientious diligence. He works exceedingly slowly, writing and rewriting each composition until it lies before him in the clearest of "fair copies," without a single correction, every page smooth and firm as a marble slab on which the tooth of time can leave no mark. The advance is also, and chiefly, due to the fact that Ibsen is a poet pure and simple, and has never wanted to be anything else. There may seem to be something cold and dead about an author who never lets himself be tempted by outward circumstances to take part in any controversy, whom no event can excite or inspire to an outburst. In all probability, the only newspaper articles Ibsen has written during the last fifteen years, are one or two on the subject of his relations with publishers, or on the powerlessness of the law to protect him against the piracy of foreign translators—all, in short, touching on his personal and private interests.

But it ought not to be forgotten that this cold reserve has permitted him to keep pre-eminence in his art ever before him as his

---

[1] Later remark. In these words lies the germ of *An Enemy of the People.*—G. B.

one idea, the goal never lost sight of—and at last reached. A more striking contrast can scarcely be imagined than that between the poet who sits solitary in the south, shut out from the world on every side, fashioning and filing into shape one artistic master-piece after another, absolutely undistracted from his calling, and his great colleague in the north, who pours into the press from full, all too full, hands, long and short articles on political, social, and religious questions, is lavish of his name, pays no attention to the prudential rule which forbids one to make one's self cheap, writes songs, makes speeches, agitates, goes from public meeting to public meeting, and is never so happy as when he stands on a platform, with thousands of friends and hundreds of opponents around him, holding the attention of the entire assembly by his daring and his art.

Henrik Ibsen resembles no other living poet, and he is influenced by none. We might perhaps mention among modern authors, two who stand in a species of very distant relationship to him, the German poets, Otto Ludwig and Friedrich Hebbel; they are, however, far less modern than he. In the ferocity of their satire, Dumas and Sardou now and then remind us of him; Sardou's Rabagas (1871) bears some resemblance to Stensgaard in *The League of Youth* (1869). In spite of the difference of their natures, there is between Ibsen and Björnson, whose name involuntarily flows from one's pen when writing of Ibsen, all the resemblance necessarily entailed by common nationality, contemporaneous activity, rivalry in treat-ment of the same subjects, and similarity of development. Ibsen's production of *The League of Youth* prompted Björnson to write plays on social subjects. After Björnson had written *A Bankruptcy*, Ibsen felt a desire to vary the treatment of the subject in *The Pillars of Society*. Björnson himself told me that he had to erase a sentence in the manuscript of *Dust*, because it appeared almost word for word in Ibsen's *Ghosts*, which came out before *Dust* was printed. The fact is that the two poets have passed through an exactly similar process of development. Henrik Ibsen succeeded in escaping a little sooner than Björnson from the domain of saga, history, and fancy; situated more independently, with no home connections, and standing, as he did, right in the stream of the ideas of his age, he had less to restrain him from following the call of that age,

F

less native simplicity, and less pious reverence. That the one poet deserted the essentially romantic and took to the essentially realistic treatment of his subjects a few years before the other, in no way detracts from the wonderful parallelism in the stages of their literary development. It seems to me that Björnson and Ibsen may be compared to the two old Norwegian kings, Sigurd and Eystein, who, in the famous legendary conversation appropriated by Björnson in *Sigurd Jorsalfar*, boast to each other of their merits. The one has stayed at home and civilised his country, the other has left it, wandered far and wide, and gained honour for it on his wild and arduous journeyings. Each has his admirers, each his contentious band of followers, who exalt the one at the expense of the other. But they are brothers, although they have for a time been at variance; and the only right thing to happen—and it does happen at the end of the play—is the peaceable division of the kingdom between them.

THIRD IMPRESSION

(1898)

THIRD IMPRESSION

(1898)

SIXTEEN years ago, it was natural to conclude a characterisation of Ibsen with a comparison between him and Björnson. Since then Ibsen has developed so steadily and powerfully, and has soared so high in his poetic flight, that he has far out-distanced all rivals both at home and abroad. His fame has in the literal sense of the word become world-wide. In French and English, and possibly also in other languages, such words as "Ibsenism" and "Ibsenite" have been coined from his name; no other Scandinavian poet or author occupies the attention of the age as he does; on the threshold of old age, he still holds his place in the intellectual vanguard, so that his works are opposed, ridiculed, loved, and worshipped, as only a young or comparatively young man's generally are.

The features of his intellect have undergone no material alteration during the last sixteen years; they were too strongly marked for that; but new traits have been added, and the whole expression has become even more instinct with genius than it was. It has, moreover, been the privilege of the writer of these lines to become acquainted with one or two of Ibsen's unpublished, or at any rate quite unknown, early works, which throw a new light on some of his well-known dramas of the same period.

I

IN the year 1850, while Henrik Ibsen was preparing for his matriculation examination, he completed, during his Whitsuntide holidays, a little one-act play, *The Hero's Grave*, which was performed at the Christiania Theatre in September and October of the same year, three times in all. It was never independently published, but in 1854 it appeared in a revised form as a *feuilleton* in a Bergen newspaper. Twice again, in January 1854 and February 1856, it was acted at the Christiania Theatre.

If one did not know who was the author of this work, one would never guess it from the work itself: Ibsen is still so dependent on his first models. The metre, the choice of words, the whole strain of the language no less than the subject, the conception of the ancient Scandinavians, all the emotions and ideas, reveal a young and enthusiastic disciple of the then aged Oehlenschläger. The well-written, easy-flowing verses have the Oehlenschläger rhythm and ring, the figures seem to have stepped out of an Oehlenschläger tragedy or tragic idyll.

In respect to poetical tradition, the critical instinct had not, at this early period, awakened in Henrik Ibsen. He shared the established views. The interest of the play turns on the warm enthusiasm for the North, the North of ancient days, which the poet has depicted as existing in the breast of a young Southern girl. The young Ibsen perhaps accentuates more sharply than Oehlenschläger is in the habit of doing, the coarseness and cruelty attendant on the Viking expeditions; yet he sees them in a most poetical light, a light which falls upon them very strongly in the devotion of the fair young foreigner to the Northern heroes. Blanka in this play, fascinated by the exploits of the blue-eyed sea-kings, dreams of the North, longs for the North, in much the same way in which the young English girl, Miss Carteret, in Oehlenschläger's *Tordenskjold*, lives a life of rapturous devotion to the Danish naval hero whom she has never seen, and Maria in *The Varangians* adores Harald Haardraade.

The play seems to convey the idea that the vigorous life of that time had deserted the South to flourish in the North.   In the South it had long ago flowered in glorious deeds and in great works of art; now life there was "chiselled and painted," as the poem says; but in the North, where nature was stern and art not yet in existence, it pulsated strongly.   But this was precisely Oehlenschläger's view as well.

In Ibsen, however, the exaltation of Northern heathenism at the expense of Southern Christianity is not so striking as in Oehlenschläger's *Earl Hakon, Palnatoke,* and *The Varangians.* Blanka's praying for her enemies astounds the heathen prince. In vain does the young Northerner attempt to steel himself against the strong impression made by this superior excellence.   Oehlenschläger's Auden (Odin) in *Earl Hakon,* addressing Olaf Trygvason, the introducer of Christianity, uses the famous words—

"Boy, let my fir-trees stand!"

Ibsen's Gandolf replies in the same strain to Blanka, when she declares that if her faith were planted in northern soil, flowers would cover the naked mountain sides—

"Let the mountain stand
With naked sides, until time levels it."

But Blanka triumphs, and in her person the spirit of a new age accompanies the sea-king to his home.   By her influence his character is softened and ennobled.   In this play, then, goodness is the ideal; not strength, but goodness is the greatest thing in the world in Ibsen's eyes when he is twenty-two, as in Oehlenschläger's when he was seventy.   To Ibsen at a later period the goodness ideal, pure and simple, becomes more debatable, as Aunt Julia in *Hedda Gabler* shows us.

Faintly outlined as he is, the old Viking who has been left on the distant island, and who at last determines to end his days there, is also an Oehlenschläger figure, reminding us slightly of the hero in *The Two Bracelets.*   The bard determining to remain with him, in order to close his eyes and sing his Drapa (deathsong), is a touch of good old romance.

But, in spite of all this imitativeness, the very young poet's awakening individuality finds expression in the last lines of the

play, when Blanka prophesies that, as the hero rises to Valhalla
from his burial-mound,

> "So, too, the North will from its tomb arise
> To scour the sea of thought, on high emprise!"

The lines containing this somewhat irrelevant prophecy are, signi-
ficantly enough, the only lines in Ibsen's own hand in the MS. of
the play preserved in the library of the Bergen theatre. In them
he has unmistakably expressed his strong and justified faith in
the future.

As *The Hero's Grave* shows what a deep impression Oehlenschläger's northern tragedies made on Henrik Ibsen's young
mind, so *Olaf Liliekrans* and *The Feast at Solhaug* furnish a
proof that until his thirtieth year he looked upon the mediæval
heroic ballad as a desirable source of inspiration for the modern
dramatic poet.

Olaf Liliekrans was sketched and already commenced in 1850,
but it was not completed until 1856; it was performed at the
Bergen theatre twice, on the 2nd and 4th January 1857.

Until it began to attempt to reflect the actual life of the
time, all modern Danish-Norwegian poetry and fiction derived
its inspiration from three literary sources—the Icelandic Edda
or Saga literature, the national ballads, and Holberg. Henrik
Ibsen, like other Scandinavian writers, was at first influenced by
all three.

No one who is unacquainted with the Scandinavian languages
can fully understand the charm that the style and melody of the
old ballads exercise upon the Scandinavian mind. The beautiful
ballads and songs of *Des Knaben Wunderhorn* have perhaps had
a similar power over German minds, but, as far as I am aware, no
German poet has ever succeeded in inventing a metre suitable for
dramatic purposes, which yet retained the mediæval ballad's
sonorous swing and rich aroma. The explanation of the powerful
impression produced in its day by Henrik Hertz's *Svend Dyring's
House* is to be found in the fact that in it, for the first time, the
problem was solved of how to fashion a metre akin to that of the
heroic ballads, a metre possessing as great mobility as the verse
of the Nibelungenlied, along with a dramatic value not inferior to
that of the iambic pentameter. Henrik Ibsen, it is true, has

justly pointed out that, as regards the mutual relations of the principal characters, *Svend Dyring's House* owes more to Kleist's *Käthchen von Heilbronn* than *The Feast at Solhaug* owes to *Svend Dyring*. But the fact still remains that the versified parts of the dialogue of both *The Feast at Solhaug* and *Olaf Liliekrans* are written in that imitation of the tone and style of the heroic ballad, of which Hertz was the happily-inspired originator. There seems to me to be no depreciation whatever of Ibsen in this assertion of Hertz's right to rank as his model. Even the greatest must have learnt from some one.

One great interest of *Olaf Liliekrans* lies in the testimony it affords to the strength of Ibsen's enthusiasm for the spirit and tone of the heroic ballad, though along with this we have here and there a hint of his instinctive scepticism with regard to the world of romance in which tradition still holds him spell-bound. He has on this occasion assimilated various romantic elements. There is first the ballad of Sir Olaf, who is lured away by the fairy as he is setting out to bring home his bride—one of the most favourite mediæval ballads, the source of inspiration of Heiberg's *Fairy Hill*, Gade's *Fairy Spells*, &c., &c. Then there is the story of the young girl, "The Ptarmigan of Justedal" (which was the original title of *Olaf Liliekrans*), who at the time of the plague was the only human being left alive in Justedal valley, and who lived there, solitary and shy as a ptarmigan, until she was found, educated, and happily married.

The diction of this poem, and of all Ibsen's youthful works in the original editions, is purely Danish ; hardly a dozen distinctively Norwegian words occur in the whole play, and there is not a single un-Danish turn of phrase—facts which strengthen one's impression that we have here to do with a youthful disciple of the Danish school of poetry. The verses are smooth and flowing, without any marked peculiarity. The value of the piece as a play, however, is not great. The principal character, Sir Olaf, exhibits throughout a youthful, almost pitiable, dependence on his mother, and consequent irresoluteness ; and partly because of Olaf's lack of energy, partly by reason of Ibsen's inclination as a young dramatist to produce complications by misunderstandings and mistakes, the situation is worked up by purely external means. The heroine, Alfhild, appears decked as a bride in the expectation that she is about to be married to her lover, who has not disclosed to her his faint-hearted return to his former betrothed, whom he is to marry that very evening. A catastrophe ensues, in the shape of the half-deranged Alfhild's attempted incendiarism, and her flight. To all appearance ruin and the punishment of death await the incendiary, but a happy solution of the difficulties is found, and two couples are united in marriage.

The romance in this youthful work of Ibsen's is of much less significance to us to-day than those traits which point forwards, across the romantic period in the poet's life, towards the keenly satirical or bitterly pessimistic poetry of the future. Several such traits are to be found in the last two acts.

Alfhild is the daughter of the minstrel Thorgjerd, a dweller on the upland wastes. Her father has inoculated her from childhood with his poetically idealised views of life and death, especially of death. He has taught her that death is nothing but a bright spirit who releases the sorrowing and suffering mortal from all his woes, and prepares for him a couch of lilies and roses, on which he is wafted to heaven, where he lives on in joy and glory. As early as in the second act, she discovers that death is not this at all, but the grave and desolation ; and after a pause, she remarks quietly and thoughtfully—

" Death in my father's lays was not like this."

There is something in the way in which reality is here contrasted with fantastic illusion that presages *Peer Gynt*, and also something here and there in the construction and swing of the verse in the romantic-lyrical passages that anticipates the strain in which Peer Gynt, as a youth, rehearses his poet's and liar's dreams. The following passage distinctly recalls certain lines in the episode of Peer Gynt's visit to the Dovrë King :—

" 'Tis true ; all this wealth of mirth and cheer
No one knows of down here.
Of the elf-king's hoard have you never been told,
That shines each night like the ruddy gold?
But if you try to lay hands on't, alas !
You'll find you're clutching at weeds and grass.
And listen, Alfhild—it well may be,
That life's like the elf-king's treasury !

> Go not too close to it, for fear
> Those little fingers you chance to sear.
> 'Tis true it shines like the starry sky
> When seen from afar; but come not nigh!"

Still more significant is the passage in the third act, where Ingeborg and Heming have fled from home, each to escape from a hated marriage, with the intention of leading an idyllic life on the mountain wilds. They are to support themselves by hunting and fishing. But it turns out that Heming has neither bow nor fishing-lines, and that Ingeborg cannot get on without her maids, without society, without dance and song. Neither of them can exist except in the society they have just left. Neither of them is capable, even for one day, of seeing in love the enduring and sustaining power that will make them forget all privations. There is here a foreshadowing of the situation of Falk and Svanhild in *Love's Comedy*, after Guldstad has shown Svanhild the importance of creature comforts and worldly well-being.

It is highly probable that the passages quoted did not occur in the original form of the play, but were inserted in 1856.

The minstrel Thorgjerd's last speech is genuinely Ibsenish. A chord vibrates throughout it which the poet has touched more than once in his songs, when describing the homelessness and unrest attendant on his fateful vocation:—

> " A minstrel has neither house nor home,
> He never can rest, for his heart bids him roam.
> Whoso bears a treasure of song in his breast,
> He is homeless in the east, he is homeless in the west.
> In the green spring vale, on the leaf-crowned hill,
> He must sing, he must make the harp-strings thrill.
> He must waylay the life that lurks secretly
> In the torrent-swept rock and the wind-washed sea;
> Must waylay the life in each heart's pulsation,
> Clothe the people's visions in melody,
> And clear their thoughts' fermentation."

Olaf Liliekrans now exists only in the manuscript from which it was acted at the Bergen theatre forty-one years ago.[1] The

---

[1] *Olaf Liliekrans* and *The Hero's Grave* are soon to appear in the complete popular edition of Ibsen's works now in course of publication in Copenhagen. German translations of them have already appeared in Vol. II. cf *Henrik Ibsen's Sämtliche Werke*. Berlin: S. Fischer, 1898.

play did not greatly please the local critics, and can scarcely have satisfied its author, since he has never taken any steps towards publishing it. Now, when every stage in his development is of importance to us, the old play presents no small historic and psychological interest. Just as *Catilina* marks his point of departure as a revolutionary, so *Olaf Liliekrans* marks his point of departure as a romanticist, and at the same time indicates his first doubts of that romance which disregards experience and reality.

Olaf Liliekrans leads us up to *The Feast at Solhaug*.

In the preface to the second edition of the latter play, Henrik Ibsen has given such a full account of its origin and its first reception, that hardly anything remains to be said. Who can understand the origin of a work, the internal and external causes that produced it, so well as its creator? And how imperfect is everything that another can say about it, in comparison with a frank and exhaustive statement by the author!

We can only wish that Ibsen had given us a similar history of the origin of all his works.

His statement, however, is perhaps not altogether exhaustive. Both as a poet and as a human being he is far too reserved for that. In his preface he only touches lightly on the fact that behind the poetical emotions and literary theories that gave birth to this composition, there lay personal experiences. Speaking of the reasons that led him to write this lyric-romantic play before the previously-planned *Vikings*, he says quite briefly: " Most of them, and presumably the strongest and most decisive, were of a personal nature; but I think, too, that my careful study of Landstad's collection of Norwegian folk-songs and ballads about this time was not altogether without significance." That strong influences of a private and personal nature had been at work could be divined from the matter of the play, especially as the same theme recurs several times in Ibsen's youthful writings, notably in *The Vikings*, published two years later.

It is not for a critic who has received no private information whatever from the author, to say where the personal element comes in. He can only point out that the play is young, that it affects the senses like youthful, emotional music, and that youthful experiences must lie behind it—experiences such as few gifted young men escape. There is the young, passionate woman, whom the youth has known and felt drawn to when she was yet half a child, and whom he meets again when she has married another, has been disappointed in her marriage, and still cherishes the memory of the friend of her early youth. There is the contrast between the two women, the one passionate, maddened, tempting and tempted to crime, the other artlessly loving and devoted. Finally, the chief male character is a poet. He had sung himself into Margit's heart, as he three years afterwards sings himself into Signe's. And he is an outlawed poet, outlawed as Ibsen must long have felt himself to be, and homeless, as Thorgjerd in *Olaf Liliekrans* was homeless. The theme of *The Feast at Solhaug* is fate's disentanglement of the young knight and singer from the net wound round him by the first fancy he has aroused in a woman's heart.

The little poem is beautifully rounded off, harmonious and complete, with no irrelevant detail, and every action psychologically motived. The increasing agony of mind that brings Margit to the brink of crime is depicted with unerring dramatic power. The powers of darkness that possess her soul are made transparently clear to us. Indeed, all the characters have the quality of transparence; they are like the figures in a painted window, warm in colour, clear and bright, lightly and yet quite distinctly outlined. The most elaborated one is the only one that has a slightly comical touch about it, approaching caricature—Margit's husband, the worthy, stupid, narrow-minded, tactless knight, Bengt. In him we dimly discern the prototype of George Tesman in *Hedda Gabler*.

The play is written in alternating verse and prose, the transitions so skilfully managed that there is never the least awkwardness. From the most commonplace dialogue, the language rises to lyric fervour and the impetus of passion. The conclusion of the second act, with the song in which Gudmund rejects Margit's love, and the story in which Margit depicts the anguish the slight causes her, reveals the future master of indirectly-expressed emotion and dramatic contrast.

We feel that *The Feast at Solhaug* is written by a young romanticist, who has purposely deprived his subject of its tragic sting in order that all may end in lyric calm, but in whom, nevertheless, dwells the spirit of the tragedian who will become great only on the day when merciless love of truth has made him indifferent to all cheap final harmony.

Lady Inger, which was written in Bergen in the winter of
1854, performed for the first time at the Bergen theatre on
January 2, 1855, printed (only a few copies) in 1857, finally
published in a slightly revised form in 1874, and afterwards
performed in Norway, Sweden, Finland, and Germany, is,
beyond comparison, the best of the works produced by Henrik
Ibsen before his thirtieth year. The subject is Norwegian and
patriotic, and the play was written for the anniversary of the
foundation of the Bergen Theatre. It is evidently an expression
of the young poet's warm patriotic feeling, and it is not surprising
that its sting should be directed against Denmark; this lay partly
in the nature of the play, partly in the antagonistic attitude
towards everything Danish which Norwegian national feeling
assumed as long as the Danish accent prevailed on the stage of the
Christiania Theatre, and emancipation from this and other tradi-
tions of the Danish period was being aimed at.

Historical in as far as the names of the characters are concerned, the play does not in any particular represent actual
historical circumstances and events. The real Lady Inger was
not a representative of the anti-Danish movement in Norway;
she had nothing whatever to suffer from the marriage of her
daughters with Danish noblemen; the "Dalejunker" (the Nils
Stensön of the play), to whom she betrothed one of her daughters,
was not her son, and was not even Sten Sture's, although she
thought he was. Nils Lykke, to whom Ibsen has transferred
certain traits which in song and legend are attributed to the
Danish nobleman, Kai Lykke, was not the irresistible seducer of
the play, but was first married to Lady Inger's daughter Eline,
and, after her death, had a liaison with her second daughter,
Lucia, which, according to the views of that period, was regarded
as incest, and resulted in his imprisonment and death.

Ibsen has re-cast all these characters and circumstances. Out
of nothing he has created a national heroine, whose mission it
is to set her country free, but who, by an unhappy fate, feels
herself continually checked and hampered in carrying out her
purpose by her fears for her illegitimate son, exposed, as a kind
of hostage, to the enemy's vengeance. Ibsen has succeeded in
endowing this figure with tragic grandeur. Then, out of his own
imagination, he has modelled the other principal character, the
Danish knight, Nils Lykke, the ambitious diplomatist and clever

intriguer, whose power over the young women who cross his path has become proverbial among his contemporaries. This figure is perhaps less original than the first, but it possesses inward coherence, clearness of outline, vigorous life, and it stands firmly on its feet. Finally, he has here produced his first fascinating and touching female character, the young Eline Gyldenlöve, at first so proud and firm, then so rapidly and completely carried away by her passionate love.

Here were the elements of a direct and simple tragedy. Ibsen has constructed with them a drama of intrigue, in which new complications are constantly arising, and the characters grope their way through darkness, in which they are kept by the will of the poet, in order that they may go astray again and again. They are entangled in a web of misunderstandings, which, when it is rent asunder at any one point, is twined more closely round them at another, so as to force them to act with desperate inexpediency. The poet has shrunk from no improbability in order to allow of this blind action on the part of his characters; Eline Gyldenlöve, for instance, is fully acquainted with the circumstances of her dead sister's fate, yet has no idea of the name of the man who wrought her destruction, and is almost to the last unaware that it was Nils Lykke, the man she loves. A consistent mystery - mongering is carried on throughout the play, which alone makes the misunderstandings possible; it is here for the first time that Ibsen reveals himself as the ingenious mystifier he still is. Behind the almost too dextrous art with which the threads of the plot are twisted, one already feels the expert, the stage-manager, whose study of foreign, especially French plays, and whose daily experience, have given him an unerring perception of what is effective on the stage.

At the very beginning of the play, for instance, Olaf Skaktavl comes to Östraat, knowing that he is to meet a man there, but ignorant as to who the man is. Nils Lykke, who expects to meet Count Sture, hearing that a stranger has arrived, naturally takes Skaktavl to be Sture, while Skaktavl, who is to meet Nils Stenssön, is bound to conclude that Nils Lykke is he. Although the Danish knight does not know whom he is addressing, he cunningly represents himself to Skaktavl to be the man the latter expected to meet. Then Nils Stenssön appears on the scene. He too is to meet a stranger at Östraat, who has not been very accurately described to him, but to whom he is to deliver papers and letters. Nils Lykke fraudulently succeeds in getting these papers, which were meant for Olaf Skaktavl, delivered to himself, and thus becomes acquainted with secrets, the possession of which gives him the advantage over the others, an advantage which is doubled when Lady Inger involuntarily reveals to him the fatal secret of her life.

When the darkness has begun to disperse, when Nils Lykke not only knows that Nils Stenssön is Sten Sture's and Lady Inger's son, but has also imparted this knowledge to the young man, who had previously known neither of his parents, and when the plot seems to be approaching its dénouement without other complications than those which arise from the existing situation, in combination with the characters of the personages, all suddenly becomes dark again. For Nils Stenssön's tongue is tied by a promise of silence that Nils Lykke has extracted from him, so that the son does not tell his mother who he is, and the ambitious mother, who has never seen her darling child (a somewhat improbable supposition), takes him to be the rival aspirant to the throne, and causes him to be assassinated.

Finally, in order to intensify the suspense, Ibsen has had recourse to an expedient to which he has frequently recurred in his later plays, in spite of its being scarcely justifiable from an artistic point of view, and condemned even by Aristotle in his Poetics : namely, keeping not only the actors but also the spectators as long as possible in ignorance of the real antecedents and conditions of the action. The exposition, which is excellent in every other respect, does not enlighten the spectators in the very least as to what is the secret that hampers Lady Inger's patriotic energy. They do not learn it until late, almost too late.

In spite of these peculiarities and defects, and in spite of some prolixity of dialogue, there is great power and tragic grandeur in this drama. The simplest scenes are the most beautiful. Nils Stenssön's youthful figure, which comes tumbling into the plot with such humorous effect, and which has more freshness about it than Oehlenschläger's parallel figure, Oluf, in *Queen Margarethe*, brings with it a breath of careless youth ; and the love-scenes between Eline and Nils Lykke are unforgetable in virtue of the poetic, overpowering passion of the noble maiden, which is so quickly awakened, and which, by reason of what has gone before, only brings disaster in its train.

The chief character, Lady Inger, clearly exemplifies (most clearly, however, in the earliest edition of the play) the belief which is constantly expressed throughout Ibsen's writings, that every pre-eminent human being has a vocation, to which he is called and consecrated by God or nature, which he dares not abandon, and cannot fulfil without great sacrifice of inclinations, feelings, and pleasures, which, but for this vocation, he might permit himself and others. Lady Inger is hampered by her maternal affection. She has sinned against her vocation by bringing a son into the world whose existence she must conceal. Observe how this genuinely poetical, half religious or theological belief in a vocation finds reiterated expression in *The Pretenders, Brand, Peer Gynt, Emperor and Galilean, An Enemy of the People, Rosmersholm, The Master-Builder,* &c. It has probably been the strongest stay of Ibsen's own inner life. Very significant in this respect is the expression of which he makes use in a petition to King Carl in the year 1866, referring to what he regarded as his poet's vocation—"that life-work which I firmly believe and know that God has given me to do."

G

IN the "Second Impression" we traced Ibsen's development up to the period at which *An Enemy of the People* was written.

The hostile reception encountered by that remarkable and profound play, *Ghosts*, made an unusually deep impression upon Henrik Ibsen, who had had reason to consider his reputation established. Almost all the copies sent to Norway from Copenhagen were returned unsold, and the Norwegian Liberal press vied with the Conservative in attacks on the play and its author. In Denmark the Conservative press raged furiously against *Ghosts*.

That the attitude which Ibsen's own countrymen assumed towards him on this occasion affected him painfully is shown by the circumstance that, contrary to his custom, both before and after this time, of publishing a play only every other year, he had by the end of one year completed the drama, *An Enemy of the People*, which, as has been already indicated, adumbrates the spiteful reception accorded to *Ghosts*. *An Enemy of the People* represents the infamous treatment to which a high-principled and able man, the doctor at the mineral-water baths of a little Norwegian town, is subjected, when he discovers and makes it known that the water-supply of the place is fatally contaminated. The doctor, in his simplicity, has hoped that this discovery, along with his carefully thought out plan for remedying the evil, will earn for him the gratitude of his fellow-townsmen. At first it seems as if this were to be the case. For a moment it appears as though the opposition party meant to support him, in order to use him against the party in power. But the town will not run the risk of even temporarily getting into bad repute as a watering-place; its inhabitants are afraid of frightening away visitors; they will not incur the great expense which a thorough re-arrangement of their water-supply system would entail, and unanimously prefer to throw overboard the doctor, who will not let himself be cajoled or frightened into silence.   Indeed, they not merely throw him overboard, but do so with violence, shouting him down, loading him with abuse, and even attacking his house with stones.

The present generation has reason to be grateful to those who in their stupidity or hypocrisy attacked *Ghosts*, and prevented its performance, for having thus provoked Ibsen to write *An Enemy of the People*.   The play is one of his keenest and wittiest, and he has succeeded admirably in keeping the character of Dr. Stockmann distinct from himself, and giving it independent life, even though he does make the courageous and humorous physician very plainly his own mouthpiece in the great speech of the fourth act.

In *An Enemy of the People*, the poet's essentially aristocratic principles are for the first time clearly enunciated—aristocratic principles which by no means exclude a friendly feeling towards the masses, and desire for their elevation.   Never before had he so forcibly preached the doctrine that the majority is always in the wrong.   The play, indeed, concludes with the Kierkegaard-like paradox : "The strongest man in the world is he who stands [most] alone."[1]   Not since he wrote *Brand* had Ibsen followed so closely in Kierkegaard's footsteps as he does here.   But that which, in the case of the great thinker who died a generation before this drama came into existence, was a doctrine exemplified in a life, finds its expression here in the interplay of a number of lifelike figures, conceived with a humour and bitter satire unsurpassed by Kierkegaard himself.

After *An Enemy of the People* came *The Wild Duck*, a masterpiece, and perhaps the most pessimistic play that Ibsen had yet written ; though even a character of such a low type as Gina, who had been old Werle's mistress before she was married to the lazy and affected Hjalmar Ekdal, is drawn almost affectionately.   All the light of the play, however, is centred round the head of Hedvig, that pathetically lovable and noble-hearted child.   In this important work also we can trace an after-effect of the maltreatment that was Ibsen's recompense for *Ghosts*, in the character, namely, of Gregers Werle, who is a caricature of the man who insists on bearing witness

---

[1] Schiller says much the same thing in *Wilhelm Tell:*
"Der Starke ist am mächtigsten allein."—G. B.

for the truth. After having poured out the vials of his wrath, and spoken his mind freely, in *An Enemy of the People*, Ibsen seems to have asked himself for the first time if it were really worth the trouble, if it were really his duty to proclaim the truth to average people like his readers, if it were not rather falsehood that was necessary to them in the conduct of their lives. The quietly humorous spirit of his answer to this question led to the creation of Gregers Werle, an everywhere superfluous and intrusive personage, who goes from house to house urging the claim of the ideal, and only at the end of the play learns the wise lesson that if you take away all falsehood from the average man, you take happiness away from him at the same time—a truth which is imparted to Gregers by the cynically good-natured Relling, another humorous incarnation of Ibsen himself.

The high standard of excellence attained by Ibsen in *The Wild Duck*, and the progress in his art which it denotes, is best understood by comparing this drama with *The Pillars of Society*. In the earlier play we have a melodramatic ending, the conversion of the principal character, the rescue of the ship, and even of the runaway son, all meant to smooth away what is bad and horrible; here we have the beautiful and bitter reality of life, the full austerity together with the full suavity of art.

Who knows but that even in *Rosmersholm*, Ibsen's next play, there may be a hidden, masked reminiscence of that turning-point in his literary career, the fierce attack on *Ghosts?* Rosmer begins where Dr. Stockmann left off. He wants to do from the very first what the doctor only wanted to do at the end of *An Enemy of the People*—make proud, free, noble beings of his countrymen. At the beginning of the play Rosmer is believed to be a decided Conservative (which the Norwegians considered Ibsen to be for many years after the publication of *The League of Youth*), and as long as this view is generally held, he is esteemed and admired, while everything that concerns him is interpreted in the most favourable manner. As soon, however, as his complete intellectual emancipation is discovered, and especially when it appears that he himself does not attempt to conceal the change in his views, public opinion turns against him. The Conservatives begin to persecute him, and the Liberals beseech him to keep silence, as he may be of use to them by means of his prestige, whereas they have no use whatever for declared freethinkers in their camp. His relations with Rebekka, which previously to this had not given rise to any scandal whatever, and were even regarded as blameless beyond all possibility of criticism, are now found to lend themselves to suspicion in every possible way. Ibsen had been almost as much exposed as Rosmer to every sort of attack for some time after the publication of *Ghosts*, which (from the Conservative point of view) marked his conversion to radicalism.

The year before the publication of *Rosmersholm*, after an absence of eleven years, Ibsen had once more paid a visit of some weeks to Norway. From a speech he made at Trondhjem, on the occasion of a demonstration by the Workmen's Union in his honour, we learn that he had found "immense progress in most directions," but that he had also experienced disappointments, inasmuch as he found "the most indispensable individual rights" far less assured than he had expected; the individual was not granted "either religious liberty or freedom of utterance beyond an arbitrarily fixed limit." In this speech he said plainly: "Hence there remains much to be done before we can be said to have attained real liberty. But I fear that our present democracy will not be equal to the task. An element of *nobility* must be introduced into our national life, into our parliament, and into our press. Of course it is not nobility of birth that I am thinking of, nor of money, nor yet of knowledge, nor even of ability and talent: I am thinking of nobility of character, of will, of soul."

There are traces in *Rosmersholm* of the poet's newly-acquired, fresh, and unbiassed view of the party situation in Norway, and also of his feeling of the want of any noble element in the political conditions of his country. Standing head and shoulders above Kroll and Mortensgaard, those inimitable personifications of stubborn fanatical reaction and of the plebeian popular party, we see the refined, somewhat colourless face of Rosmer, that distinguished but impotent character, who lacks all the qualities which go to make the leader, but who possesses that calm nobility which was Ibsen's desideratum. The misfortune is that Rosmer succeeds in imparting this nobility only to the woman who loves him, and not to the masses who are so sadly in need of it.

This woman, Rebekka, is the principal figure in the play, and one of Ibsen's greatest, most admirable creations. He had never before equalled the sublime calm, the unerring knowledge of human nature, with which this character is represented, explained, and indirectly judged.   He whose special task it had long been to show spuriousness in the seemingly genuine, to listen for the hollow ring in the apparently solid substance, has here overcome his old distrust, and has believed in the purifying of this woman with the sullied past, has demonstrated for us the sound kernel, the purity, and in the end the greatness, which exist in this criminal, liar, and murderess.   He has accomplished this in so convincing a manner, that even he who has never met with a Rebekka—and among all Ibsen's Norwegian women she is by far the most uncommon—even he never for a moment entertains a doubt of her possibility.   Only she is more generally human than specially Norwegian; in some ways she strikes one as being Russian.

Finally, the reader must be reminded of the art with which Ibsen, towards the end of the play, employs the fantastic personality of Ulrik Brendel to break in on the emotion of the scene, and thereby intensify it.

Rebekka in *Rosmersholm* is like a personification of the Nordland whence she came, the land of extreme alternations, of unbroken darkness and uninterrupted light, the land of violent, uncontrolled temperaments.   All the similes wherewith she attempts to portray her own nature, she borrows from the stormy surroundings in which she has spent her early youth.   Her passion for Rosmer, for instance, she likens to a Nordland winter storm, resistless in its might.

The heroine in Ibsen's next play, *The Lady from the Sea*, resembles the violently agitated and changeable sea on the west coast of Norway, where she was born and brought up.   She is always longing for the sea, and, like it, she is mysterious.   A child of nature, nervous to disease, to a certain extent under hypnotic influence, on the brink of insanity, she strives unconsciously after liberty and responsibility.

In *The Lady from the Sea*, Ibsen returns to that symbolism to which he was inclined in his youth, and of which *Brand* and *Peer Gynt* are examples.   For the first time one feels decidedly, and with a certain sadness, that the polemical period in his career is at an end.   The drama has the effect of a very skilfully carried out, psychologico-fantastic experiment.   It does not pass in broad daylight, but as it were on a Rembrandt canvas, from the darkness of whose background " the Stranger," that mystical object of the feminine longing for freedom from restraint, and of the feminine fear of the unknown, suddenly emerges for a few moments, to disappear again as suddenly and for ever. The mysterious power which the strange sailor exercises over Ellida is broken from the moment that Wangel allows her her free choice.

It would be small-minded to dwell on the serious improbabilities we must accept as part of the poet's presuppositions—the character of the Stranger, his preparations for Ellida's instant flight with him, &c. Much worse than these is the conventional ending, the belief in the magic words, " Liberty, with responsibility," that change everything, though everything remains the same. There are few things less capable of calming a woman who is longing for a free, adventurous life with all its mysteries, than the offer of such moral advantages as free choice with responsibility.

The two young daughters of the house are drawn in Ibsen's most masterly style. Hilda is as yet only the half-grown girl, exuberant, rather cruel, and yet longing for love; we know that in time she becomes the marvellous heroine of *The Master-Builder*. Boletta is the young girl who feels compelled to say farewell to all the golden dreams of her youth and marry a good man, much older than herself, whom she does not love. It makes a strong impression on us that the tragedy of the parents' lives (Ellida's unsatisfactory union with the elderly Wangel) exactly repeats itself in the lives of their children. We look, as it were, along an endless vista of earthly disappointments.

With *Hedda Gabler* Ibsen once more enters the domain of realism. There is nothing emblematic here, nothing but a severely accurate analysis and synthesis of a richly endowed and meagrely developed young woman, who is at once strong and cowardly, enthusiastic and conventional, ambitious and commonplace, domineering and spiteful, old-fashioned and fashionably decadent; "in short," to quote the words of an English critic, " the young lady that five times out of ten we take in to dinner."

In *Hedda Gabler* we gain insight into a society where the informality of plain-speaking is the only form observed, and where a certain crudity of thought and speech seems to have extended to the higher classes. Even where the conversation is carried on in a kind of masonic slang that is not lacking in wit, it is devoid of all refinement. The confessions made even on the occasion of a first meeting, are of a nature that in thoroughly refined society would be withheld as long as possible. There are two young wives in this play who promptly confess to a stranger that they do not love their husbands, that they even dislike them. The vices discussed are in keeping with the rest, of the least refined description; for instance, a propensity to drink so strongly developed that its victim has become an insensate drunkard, and has fallen into a state of degradation, from which he feels that he cannot recover himself.

Norwegian society is characterised in this and other dramas as a society which lacks nobility, which lacks all aristocratic tradition. Its intellectual aristocracy, its best writers, painters, sculptors, and musicians, have for many years as a rule lived abroad. And the history of Norway as a European nation has since the beginning of the century been so peaceful and so devoid of all importance, that Ibsen has not succeeded in imparting any dignity to his principal character by making her the daughter of a Norwegian general, whose pistols are spoken of with respect. The reader knows too well that a Norwegian general is a cavalry officer, who, as a rule, has never smelt powder, and whose pistols are entirely innocent of bloodshed.

Hedda Gabler shows us plainly that this Norwegian society possesses the quality of originality, young as it is. One feels that it has almost entirely expelled whatever Danish culture had penetrated into its manners, that it has to a trifling extent filled up the lacunæ with Swedish habits and Swedish words, but that for the most part nature, the fresh Norwegian nature, has been allowed to take its way unchecked. But one also feels that to this day the very palpable originality gives an impression of something unfinished and temporary, something which has not yet acquired form.

It is certainly the custom both in Norway and Sweden for men and women in good society, who are not related in any way, to say *thou* to one another as soon as their acquaintance has become at all intimate. (In this play Lövborg says *thou* to both Hedda and Thea.) But in Sweden all who have the slightest acquaintance with one another say *thou*, for the simple reason that Swedish, like Polish, has no other pronoun of address, so that without the use of *thou* conversation can only be carried on in the third person, with tiresome circumlocutions; the *thou* has almost the same signification in Sweden that it had in ancient Rome.   In Norway, on the contrary, it only implies that familiarity into which people drop in all amorphous societies where there is no intermediate condition between the stiffest reserve and the most complete frankness.

The middle-class society of which we get a glimpse in *Hedda Gabler* lacks the attraction of refinement, but also the faults attendant on over-refinement.   It has in the last generation shown a surprising power of producing great and original natural talent, but has also shown, it must be admitted, an almost equally striking want of ability to provide this remarkable talent with adequate sustenance, and satisfactory conditions of development.

Ibsen, who has always shown Norwegian society acting as a drag on every energy begotten by it, seems in *Hedda Gabler* to have wished to show how uncommonly great natural gifts necessarily lead, in this atmosphere, to disaster and ruin.   His artistic conscientiousness has, however, never been more marked than here, and his technical virtuosity has perhaps never shone forth more brilliantly.

Hedda and Thea, in their contrast to each other, are, in a manner, familiar figures.   It has been remarked before (First Impression) that from the very first Ibsen was fond of placing a strong masculine character between two women, one fierce and one gentle, one a valkyrie, the other a ministering spirit.   Thus Catiline stands between Furia and Aurelia, Gudmund, in *The Feast at Solhaug*, between Margit and Signe, Sigurd, in *The Vikings*, between Hjördis and Dagny, and Brand between Gerd and Agnes.

And even in those early days, he placed in strong contrast to his hero a weak, inferior male character, who was at first a caricature, like Bengt in *The Feast at Solhaug*, but subsequently develops into an estimable, honourable, prosaic specimen of humanity, whose relation to the demi-god or hero is the relation of the narrow, limited nature to the genius.

Thus Hedda is, in a manner, one of Ibsen's old, romantic, legendary figures, an amazon in a modern riding habit.   George Tesman is Bengt or Gunnar in the guise of the scientific lecturer of the present day.

Hedda represents herself as the exceptional woman, the woman who cannot give up her individuality, cannot allow it to be absorbed in the oneness, noble or ignoble, of a conventional marriage, just as "The Lady from the Sea" cannot become "acclimatised" in her ordinary middle-class surroundings.

But there are coarse, low instincts in Hedda from the very first—the vulgar envy which makes her, as a child, unable to bear the sight of another little girl's beautiful thick hair, and the low curiosity and shamelessness which lead her in her early youth, like the young lady in Hans Jæger's *Christiania-Bohemia*, to stand on disgustingly confidential terms with her male "comrade," and to delight in getting him to tell low stories of his dissipated night life. Her sigh for "high life," as represented by a liveried servant, betrays her low ideal of social refinement.

She is, as she herself says, the *blasée* society woman who has made a conventional marriage, in order to be provided for; she has got a husband who might have been taken bodily out of a Von Moser farce, instead of the man of distinguished ability, with a great future, whom in her ignorance and simplicity she supposed she was marrying.

She accuses herself of cowardice, and not without reason, for she has the traditional fine lady's horror of anything that can lead to a scandal. She is so miserably greedy of power as to beguile that wretched creature, Eilert Lövborg, into drinking again, merely in order to feel her influence over a human being; and she is so miserably jealous as to destroy the book he has written during his friendship with another woman, although this other woman's only real significance for him lay in her power of keeping him from the bottle.

Hedda is thus a true type of degeneration, lacking real worth, real ability, even the ability to yield herself, body and soul, to the man she loves; she cannot even for a moment merge herself in another. She has just sufficient pride to be disgusted with her George, and to consider it horrible to have to bear him a child. Her refusal to become Brack's mistress is only due in part to her love of independence; it is almost equally due to her fear of a breach of that conventionalism which is so precious to her. And the passion for the beautiful which she possesses in common with that worthy snob, Helmer, in *A Doll's House*, is scarcely more attractive in her than it was in him.

The case standing thus, how can it greatly affect us that such a creature should throw her life away, rise from life's feast, as she says? And yet it is not merely with cold regret that we hear of her death. Ibsen has managed in spite of everything to interest us in Hedda, to make her, in some way or other, sympathetic to us. In spite of everything, she was a power.

The most interesting thing about this woman, viewed as an indication of Ibsen's development, is that her evil side is represented with so much force. For a considerable period Ibsen had given way to the habit of systematically exalting women at the expense of men. Here he has drawn a woman who is more manly than many men, in so far as she has the keenest perception of the mawkishness of the prevailing idea of goodness, but who nevertheless is a morally and spiritually unfruitful being, capable of nothing but ruining, destroying, and dying.

Along with Hedda, we have in this play a genius and a fool. The genius is Eilert Lövborg, the fool, George Tesman.

That George is a fool the reader very soon feels assured; he will scarcely be so certain that Eilert Lövborg is really a genius. Ibsen is a poet, a very great poet, and it is natural that his views on scientific subjects should be those of a poet. It is so like a poet to see the mark of genius in desertion of the paths of experience and a vague prophetic dwelling on the future. Hence, when Ibsen desires to give us an impression of Lövborg's great abilities, he makes him write on the social forces and social development of the future. Perhaps to our prosaic minds it may seem as if the most sensible utterance on the subject is that of the fool of the play: "But, dear me, we know nothing whatever about all that!" Social development of the future!—what is this but pure Bellamy, or whatever the man's name may be.

But supposing Eilert Lövborg to be far more gifted than he appears to be, supposing him to be the greatest author imaginable—a real, epoch-making genius—how can he possibly wish to read his great work to one who is his colleague only in name, and whom he despises so heartily as he despises George Tesman? Think of the vehemence with which he reproaches Hedda for having descended to the level of this man! And yet it is to him he brings, on the occasion of a first visit, the most precious creation of his brain, to beg for his opinion on it; nay, so bent is he on hearing praise from those lips, that he even takes the manuscript with him to a drinking-party, there to seek out a quiet corner where he can pour forth his innermost soul to the deeply despised George.

I understand, of course, that it is necessary he should have the manuscript with him, in order that it may be lost by him and burnt by Hedda ; but all the same——! His desire to be appreciated by George is almost as great a disfigurement of his character as his having misconducted himself towards Hedda, or as the fact that he is a lost man as soon as he has carried a single glass of cold punch to his lips. *You are no gentleman, Mr. Lövborg.*[1]

Poor fellow ! Scarcely has the breath left his body before retribution overtakes him. His despised colleague inherits first what is left of his manuscript, and then what is left of his fair friend.

There are various small improbabilities in this drama. It is not very probable, for instance, that Mrs. Elvsted should go about with the whole rough draught of Lövborg's great work in her pocket, nor yet that she should sit down to reconstruct it before the body of the man she loves has grown cold. It happens, of course, for the sake of the outlook into the future.

However, in the case of a poet of Ibsen's rank one must always be chary of declaring any important incident to be improbable, not to say impossible. At the time *Hedda Gabler* was published, two of its incidents were singled out as being specially improbable, Lövborg's losing his manuscript—a thing no one does, said the critics—and Hedda's burning the said manuscript —still less, said the critics, would any one do that. As a matter of fact two actual cases in point are known to many in Scandinavia : one in which a musician's wife, in a fit of jealous hatred, burned a symphony her husband had just completed, and another in which an author, when drunk, lost the MS. of a newly-completed novel. It may be added that both composer and author were men of mark in their profession. There is indeed scarcely any limit to what a man will do under the influence of drink, and a woman under the influence of jealousy.

There is little fault to be found with Ibsen's knowledge of human nature. He knows it so well that he conjectures possible cases correctly when they have not come within his knowledge. With his art there is still less fault to be found. In *Hedda Gabler* it is as marvellous as ever.

---

[1] This phrase in English in the original.

III

Two years after the realistic *Hedda* came that profoundly symbolical work, *The Master-Builder* (1892).

This is a play that echoes and re-echoes in our minds long after we have read it. And when we have read it once we read it again, with increasing admiration. Great in its art, profound and rich in its symbolic language—these are the words that rise to our lips; and impressed, without being touched or softened, we fall to brooding and pondering over its power.

The Master-Builder gives at one and the same time a sense of enthralment and a sense of deliverance. Ibsen's intention has been to give us by means of real characters, but in a half allegorical form, the tragedy of a great artist, who has passed the prime of life. Solness is not actually a genius; if he is meant to be one, some traits are wanting. He has the attraction for women which is one attribute of genius, and an abundance of those vices that in many persons are a consequence of the egoism which would seem to be inseparable from genius of a certain type. We are not in a position to judge of the value of his work, so must take it upon trust. It is perhaps a defect in the play that no definite artistic aim, no purely intellectual enthusiasm has been attributed to Solness, which might have atoned for his very conspicuous moral failings. He ought perhaps to have introduced a new style of architecture. As it is, he says nothing very noteworthy about his profession but the one certainly profound remark, that he cannot build houses for people he does not know. If we do see a great personality in Solness, it is partly because we go half-way to meet the dramatist, whose means are necessarily so restricted, and grant him the hypotheses he requires.

Solness's radical fault is that mixture of brutality in crushing older men, and fear of being eclipsed by the younger, from which even genius is not always exempt. He has been equipped from the very first with that artist-egoism, without which a full development of innate talent is impossible. His relations with old Brovik slightly remind us of Werle's with old Ekdal; he ruins him and afterwards takes him into his office. His relations with Ragnar slightly remind us of Thorvaldsen's with Freund. Freund was "a martyr to the claims of Thorvaldsen's artistic superiority." Thorvaldsen took light and air from his young fellow-worker, kept all orders for himself, even those he could not manage to execute, and under the mask of paternal friendship made Freund's life with him a life of suffering.

And yet Thorvaldsen was far less guilty than Solness, for he took with the right of the greater and stronger. Hilda doubts not that this is her hero's case as well; whereas Solness's behaviour to the young architect is in fact dictated by a conviction that Ragnar is a man of superior ability to himself. There is something at once fierce and cunning about Solness which the productive instinct in him has rendered uncontrollable.

In sharp contrast to this cruelty of nature (though really connected with it), we have a morbid moral self-criticism which at last develops into actual disease—a scrupulousness that sets down selfish wishes and vague hopes on its list of crimes. He is the personification of utter regardlessness of others in the struggle to maintain his place as an artist, and at the same time he personifies self-torture in his concern for the victims his development has demanded, and especially in his sorrow over the wrong he has involuntarily done his wife.

In the eyes of the world he is happy, inasmuch as unusual good fortune has attended him on the road to fame; but he suffers perpetual remorse on account of the price he has had, and still daily has, to pay for his success. Strangely enough, he owed his first step on the road to fortune to the fire which destroyed his wife's old home. It was only through this that he was "enabled to build homes for human beings." The experience that home happiness seldom falls to the lot of men of genius, if only for the reason that the wife chosen in their youth cannot keep pace with their development, is one to which Solness gives expression in the words: "That I might build homes for others I had to forego—forego for all time—the home that might have been my own." And again in this other passage, "All that I have succeeded in doing, building, creating—all the beauty, security, cheerful comfort—aye, and magnificence too . . . all

this I have to make up for, to pay for—not in money, but in
human happiness. And not with my own happiness only, but
with other people's too. . . . That is the price which my position
as an artist has cost me."

And now, reversing the position, it seems to him that just
because he has paid so dearly for his place in life, he ought to
have the exclusive right to build—the right to hold all others
down.

He had not, however, had to exert himself afresh every time
he advanced a step in his career. Like all who have accomplished
anything great, he did not do it alone. Circumstances—"helpers
and servers" as he calls them in his language—accommodated
themselves to him; he, like King Hakon before him, possessed
that power which the "Schlemihls" lack, the power of making
everything helpful to him. But as his morbidity increases, he
comes to believe that he has a mysterious power of wishing, so
that the thing wished for comes to pass; where women are concerned, it takes the form of a species of hypnotic influence without
the actual exercise of hypnotism—what he has only wished or
thought of takes real form and shape for them. It is by means
of this power that he has attracted Kaia to himself, and through
her Ragnar, whom he fears. And Ibsen leaves us in uncertainty
as to whether a similar relation has not existed between him and
the heroine of the play. It is left uncertain whether or not
Solness really kissed Hilda when she was a child. From brooding over these mysterious powers and influences, Solness has
contracted a morbid dread of being considered mad; and in this
dread lies a germ of actual insanity, which in the end shows
itself in fantastic excitement.

This man, whom we do not see at any time during the course
of the play at the zenith of his powers, once showed himself at
his best to a young girl. Hilda, as a child of twelve or thirteen,
saw him standing aloft, proud and free, placing a wreath on the
spire of the church in her native town. This incident, and his
subsequent conversation with her, have created a mysterious bond
between them. During the ten years that have passed, she has
lived in this memory; it draws her to him; she wants to claim
the kingdom which, on the day of the festival, he had promised
her in ten years' time; and she comes into the room where he
sits dreading the hostility of youth, a personification of youth that

is all faith in him, all enthusiasm for him.   She has thus a family
likeness to her step-mother Ellida, who also waits ten years
for the Stranger.   And she resembles the Stranger himself in
that she does not give Solness's marriage a thought.   In *The
Lady from the Sea* we knew her as the girl with the inborn
craving for strong emotions, for the excitement which makes one
feel that one is really living; here we learn to know her as the
girl who will not be robbed of her faith in the great master-
builder, who insists on seeing him a second time at the zenith of
his powers, alone and free.   This is symbolised in the play by her
insistence on seeing him once more place the wreath upon a high
tower.

In the meantime he has become dizzy, as dizzy as his own
conscience.   But at her coming, this dizziness must and shall
vanish.   She cannot bear to have it said with justice that *her*
master-builder dares not—cannot—climb as high as he builds.

This speech contains the central idea of the play.   In order to
understand it aright, let us for the moment express it in other
terms ; let us say, for instance : It must not be possible for any
one to say with justice that my poet in his life cannot rise to the
height of the ideals which he proclaims in his books.

Had the argument been propounded thus, the play would have
been something quite different, something more concrete, closer
to earth.   As we have it, it is more poetical, more fascinating in
its twilight ambiguity.   Much art is needed to make us so entirely
believe in the symbol that it has not the effect of a mere symbol.
In order to keep the reader in the atmosphere of the drama, Ibsen
has had to expend prodigious care in the sealing up of all its doors
and windows, so that not a breath of every-day common-sense
may penetrate into it.   Were this to happen, the spell would be
broken.   If even one of the characters were once to remark that
it is no criterion whatever of a master-builder's greatness whether
or not he turns giddy when climbing a church spire, the sentiment
and the symbolism would fall to pieces.   But everything of this
kind is excluded.

And in reality we see Hilda force Solness out of his ignoble
sphere of thought before we see her force him to the physical feat
of standing on a pinnacle, alone and free.   For she is alarmed
when she at last understands the meanness of his behaviour to
Ragnar.   She is dismayed by the things he says to her.   " Do

you want to kill me ? To take from me what is more than my life ? " And what is that ? " The longing to see you great—to see you, with a wreath in your hand, high, high up on a church tower "; and she presses the pencil into his fingers, and compels him to write a warm recommendation of his pupil. It is not use and wont with him to be so noble. But she is the power that forces him to be greater than is his use and wont.

And then, the relation between them growing ever more intimate and more hopeless, the drama culminates in Solness becoming Hilda's in the only way possible if they were not merely to meet in the cloud-kingdoms and air-castles of fancy, namely, in death.

He began by building churches, because, coming as he did from a pious country home, he looked on that as the worthiest work for a builder. When he had lost his children, he resolved not to build churches any more, only homes for human beings. Then came a time when he saw that building homes for human beings was "not worth sixpence . . . men have no use for these homes of theirs —to be happy in." He himself had no use for one. He no longer believes that happiness exists on earth, and now at last he has determined to build the one building in which he believes human happiness can be housed—the castle in the air that Hilda has demanded of him.

" I'm afraid you would turn dizzy before we got half way up."
" Not if I can mount hand in hand with you, Hilda."
" Then let me see you stand free and high up."

What need for interpretation here ? Everything is told in plain words, and with such ingenuity, that while it may all be taken literally, may captivate a child like any other exciting story, yet the double meaning of it all is perfectly apparent when it is looked at in the light of Solness's and Hilda's emotional exaltation.

He offers her the highest tower-room in his new house; but after she has come to know his wife personally, her "robust" conscience is affected in the same way as his; she cannot seize her happiness, because between her and it there stands a being on whom she has compassion. There is nothing left but the happiness of the castle in the air.

H

Aline, Solness's wife, is the only one of the subordinate characters that Ibsen has had to elaborate a little. She is the simple-minded devotee of duty, the jealous wife, the humble, pious being who eludes Solness as he eludes her. She is characterised in the vivid trait that it is not her children's death that has broken her down—she knows they are happy in heaven—no, what told most on her was the loss at the time of the great fire of all the dolls she had played with as a child. Her simplicity and perpetual misunderstanding of things are admirably brought out by Ibsen in her silly speech about the poor, devoted Kaia : " Heavens, what deceitful eyes she has ! "

The part that Aline plays is only that of a hindrance ; all the real action of the drama passes between Solness and Hilda. Its light comes from Hilda. This character, in its marked individuality, freshness, and brilliancy, outshines all the female figures of contemporary literature. Ibsen had produced no such effective character since *A Doll's House* and *Ghosts*, nor indeed any work of such superb quality, at once so natural and so preternatural.

Ever since Ibsen gave up his youthful predilections in the matter of both subject and treatment, he has been praised and attacked as a so-called " naturalist." In our day, the so-called "symbolists" have waged warfare against "naturalism." Such catchwords seldom mean much, but to Ibsen of all men they are least applicable. In his case realism and symbolism have thriven very well together for more than a score of years. The contrasts in his nature incline him at once to fidelity to fact, and to mysticism.

Because his nature and his plays abound in enigmas and mysteries, he is compelled, in order that he may be understood, to have recourse to emphases, repetitions, characteristic tricks of expression, in short, to a certain almost broad obviousness. And although devotion to reality characterises both his nature and his poetry, yet he is poet and thinker enough always to let a deeper meaning underlie the reality he represents. All his main outlines have an emblematic tendency ; behind everything we feel Ibsen's undermining scepticism with regard to the existing and accepted order of things, as well as his intrepidity in criticism ; and we rejoice to think that, deep as his doubt digs, even so high and sure does his imagination build.

The Master-Builder, which possibly marks a culminating

point in Ibsen's literary career, was followed by *Little Eyolf.*
This play, which is one of the saddest Ibsen has written, treats
of the relation of parents to a child.   The first act is admirably
constructed; its dramatic effect cannot indeed be surpassed or
even equalled in the following acts, as it ends with the child's
death.

The following lines might stand as a motto on the title-page
of the play :—

" *Rita.* We are creatures of earth after all.
" *Allmers.* But something akin to the sea and the heavens too,
Rita."

Ibsen's whole view of human nature is contained in these
words.

He has in this play, with his usual pregnant brevity, given
expression to his philosophy of life in a new suggestive phrase,
namely, " the law of change."   All human conditions are subject
to this law.   The poets of classic antiquity wrote " Metamor-
phoses," poems dealing with those transmutations of which their
mythology told them so much.   *Little Eyolf* is Ibsen's poem
on " Metamorphosis."   It is generally said that all living things
are subject to the law of development.   But the expression " law
of change " goes deeper and is more truthful; for change includes
progress and decline, expansion and contraction in a single comprehensive word.   And in this play we see human feelings formed
and transformed, we see them die out and come to life again in a
different form.

Two questions arise in our minds with reference to any
sudden calamity which breaks in on our lives.   We ask first,
what is the cause of this calamity ? or to use the theological
expression, whose is the sin ? or to put it in the terms of ethics
and law, with whom does the responsibility lie ?   Then comes
the question, what does it mean ? in theological terms, what has
been the intention ? in ethical, what use ought we to make of it,
if there is anything at all in it except pure and simple misfortune?

In the lives of the personages of this play, Eyolf's death is
one of these epoch-making calamities.

In their broodings over cause, fault, responsibility, Allmers
and Rita work back at last to the embrace during which the

child, forgotten for a moment, fell and was crippled for life ; and here the reader is struck by a Tolstoi-like aversion for the "creature of earth" and his attributes, in the ugly light which is thrown upon the strong, healthy love of man and wife. A kind of dualism has always been perceptible in Ibsen; he pleads the cause of nature, and he castigates nature with mystic morality; only sometimes nature is allowed the first voice, sometimes morality. In *The Master-Builder* and in *Ghosts* the lover of nature in Ibsen was predominant; here, as in *Brand* and *The Wild Duck*, the castigator is in the ascendant.

The second pivot of the play is the question as to the meaning, the intention in what has happened—little Eyolf's death seems so meaningless, a calamity which cannot possibly bring forth other fruit than anguish, accusations, and self-reproaches, and which can only harden and embitter the parents to the uttermost against each other. But in reality events have only the meaning and intention that we ourselves invest them with, by the construction we put on them, and the use we make of them. And in a manner as able as it is surprising, Ibsen, at the close of the play, by means of Rita's resolution, gives this incident an interpretation, this misfortune an intention. Little Eyolf has not lived and died in vain, since his death causes Rita and Allmers to undertake a great philanthropic work among other people's children.

Among the characters, Rita is the truest and most uncommon. No one who had not a profound knowledge of the human heart could have produced this type of jealous feminine avidity. Allmers interests us less; he is of a finer nature than Rita, but also weaker in his intellectual sterility; he is, moreover, less magnanimous than she, cannot control his sorrow, and is mean and sophistical in his attack on the broken-hearted woman.

Among the other personages Death appears, in the fantastic and unforgetable form of the Rat-Wife. She is the legendary "Pied Piper," converted into an old woman; and there is a spectral awe about the scene in which she appears.

Ibsen's latest play was published in 1896.

John Gabriel Borkman is the son of the miner to whom, according to Ibsen, rich treasures beckoned from the darkness of the mountain depths, and who penetrated to their innermost recesses.[1] As a child he heard the ore sing in the mines, when

[1] An allusion to Ibsen's poem, "Bjergmanden" (The Miner).

it was loosened; it sang for joy that it was to come to the light
of day; and John Gabriel early dreamt of becoming the liberator
of all the wealth that field and mountain and forest and sea contain.   He would awaken all the slumbering spirits of gold.   He
felt an irresistible vocation to set free all the hundreds of millions
that lay in the depths of the mountains throughout the whole
land, calling to him to put them in circulation.   He had the feeling that he alone heard the cry.   And he loved all this wealth
that demanded life of him, loved it, and the power and glory
following in its train.

For he was fascinated, spellbound, by the power as much as
by the wealth.   He aimed at gaining control over all the sources
of power in his native country; and while he lived his miner's
life, striving to get all the veins of ore throughout the land
hammered out, and all the shining gold turned to account, he
at the same time strove to create power for himself, and thereby
well-being for thousands of others.

This is the explanation he himself gives of his character.   In
reality, passion for power and an imperative desire for action
were the prime movers in his conduct; concern for the well-being
of the many followed after, as a secondary consideration.   He
began in his youth by sacrificing the happiness of the woman he
loved to the prospect of power for himself; he sought to bargain
her away to a man whose services he required.   In the hope of
attaining his great object, he then risked everything that his
position as head of a bank made it possible for him to dispose of,
the funds of the bank, the fortunes of relations and friends, the
savings of strangers, even valuables entrusted to his care; and
when a supposed friend disclosed the wild speculation that he
was carrying on, there was a total collapse, and he had to pay for
his reckless audacity by eight years' imprisonment, which were
followed by eight years more of voluntary confinement.

He had always something of the poet in his nature, and during
his long isolation, he develops into a visionary.   He no longer
lives in the world of reality, but in dreams and hopes.   He
imagines that the day of reparation is at hand, that people have
gradually come to appreciate him, that they miss him, and cannot
get on without him; and when there comes a knock at his door,
he at once strikes an attitude to receive the expected deputation.

Borkman is a Solness whom fortune has deserted; he is a

Bernick minus the meanness and hypocrisy, though like Bernick, from considerations of wealth and influence, he sacrifices the happiness of one sister and marries the other. (It may be remarked in parenthesis, that it is strange how frequently the theme of a man's relations to two sisters occurs in Ibsen's plays— we have it as far back as *Catilina*, then in *Lady Inger of Östraat*, then in *The Pillars of Society*, and now here.) We are even sometimes faintly reminded of *The Wild Duck*. The dream-life that Borkman leads in the upper story of the Rentheim family mansion suggests a reminiscence of what went on in the wild-duck's loft, and Borkman compares himself to a wounded bird.

Was he ever really great? Ibsen's intention seems to be to represent him as originally a man of extraordinary powers. If this be the case, we ought perhaps to have some better guarantee for his powers than his own words and his own overweening self-confidence. None of the other characters in the play vouch for Borkman's genius. We have only his own assertions to go by, and it must always be a difficult task for the actor to give them the additional weight imparted by intelligent interpretation. Borkman's own words do not convince me, for one, that he has ever possessed true genius; and if he lacks that, the sympathy which he requires from the spectator will necessarily be greatly diminished. He calls himself, it is true, an exceptional man, in whom unusual conduct is permissible; he talks of the curse which "we exceptional, chosen people have to bear," that of being mis-understood by the average man. He has, moreover, a strong conviction of the wonderful things he could have accomplished, *if*, &c., and of what he could still accomplish, *if only*, &c. But genius does not use the words "if" and "if only." This is the language of the unfortunates who mistake themselves for geniuses; the legion of the unsuccessful men of medium ability, in whom nothing is really great but their vanity.

Perhaps a critic has a quicker ear than others for the hollow ring in Borkman's outburst of self-esteem—for a critic is a physician in the great hospital for sick and wounded vanities, who has spent his life wading in them, wandering about among them, listening to their complaints, their boastings, all the utter-ances of their self-importance. He is not disposed to credit any man with true genius who has failed in doing the work of a genius, and has only succeeded in acquiring the inhumanity, the inconsiderateness, the indifference to the life-work of others which genius is commonly credited with, which one sometimes has to forgive or overlook in it, and which, in any case, is the easiest part of it to acquire, yet the part from which the true genius is often exempt.   Not a few of the greatest geniuses have also been the best of men, in whom intellect by no means excluded heart.

It must remain doubtful how great a measure of genius Henrik Ibsen desired to ascribe to his hero.   There are passages where the poet clearly enough takes precautions against the possible over-appreciation of Borkman's abilities.   Commercial geniuses do not generally naïvely confide their most important secrets to an untrustworthy friend, and can usually carry on their operations without making free with property entrusted to them.   A gleam of melancholy satire falls upon Borkman when he speaks of feeling " like a Napoleon who has been maimed in his first battle," and the poor unsuccessful poet and supernumerary clerk answers that he feels just the same.   There is only this difference between them, that while the poor clerk is at times unable to withstand the " horrible doubt" that he has bungled his life for the sake of a delusion, Borkman, though he may occasionally in past days have had doubts of his good fortune, has never had any doubt of his ability, and just as little of his right ; the destroyer of at least one life declares complacently, " I never do any one injustice."   However, if he has done wrong, he has also atoned for it to the uttermost.

It seems as though no more events were possible in the life of the once great banker ; and yet Ibsen's drama presents to us a whole series of catastrophes which precede his death.

For years the two sisters, his early love, Ella Rentheim, and his wife, Gunhild, have not seen one another.   For years he has not seen Ella Rentheim.   For years he has not seen his wife either ; for though she lives in the same house, she shuns and hates him on account of the dishonour he has brought upon their name, upon her, and upon her son.   In the first act we have the meeting between the two sisters, in the second act, the meeting between Ella and Borkman, in the third act the first conversation between Borkman and his wife ; and these three principal scenes, which were prescribed by the nature of the plot, are all executed with the same consummate skill.   From

time immemorial few situations have been so effective on the
stage as meetings after long separation.   And here we have
three directly and inevitably following one another.

There is in reality a fourth, namely, Ella's meeting with
Borkman's son, Erhart, whom, in the family's worst days, she
had taken and educated as her adopted son, but whom the mother
had claimed again on the completion of his fourteenth year.   He
is now twenty-three, and is the central point in the action of the
play.   The two sisters contend for him with jealous affection.
The hard mother makes an idol of him, and has high-handedly
determined that he is to become a shining light, in the brightness
of whose renown the father's shame will be forgotten ; the adoptive mother, a rare and proud character, comes, knowing herself
to be dying, to spend her last days near him, her one aim, however, being his happiness.   The struggle between the two sisters
for the youth's affections is a hard one.   Towards the end of the
play we have the father also making an appeal to his son ; after
all the years he has wasted in inactivity, he dreams of regain-
ing a position for himself, and desires his son's assistance in
doing so.

Ibsen was early and deeply engrossed by the subject of the
relations between parents and their children, especially the
relations of father and son.   In *The Pillars of Society*, at the
moment when Bernick believes that he has lost his son, his Olaf,
he recognises that he has " never really possessed " him.   Allmers,
in *Little Eyolf*, acknowledges in the self-same words that he has
" never really possessed " his own child.   The parents did nothing
to win him.   The same proves to be the case here ; neither
mother, nor adoptive mother, nor father, own their son.   But
whereas in the earlier plays this is represented as exclusively the
fault of the parents, the conception of the position here is quite
different—it goes far deeper.   It is true that Mrs. Borkman, like
Allmers, is determined to make use of her son for her own purposes, without giving any consideration to what ought to be
decisive, the bent of the young man's own nature.   But the
parents here, and especially the adoptive mother, are more
serious-minded, have far more ability and strength of character
than the son.   The demands made on him by his elders produce
no impression on his insignificance, his youthful, pleasure-loving
nature.   He will neither be a genius, as his mother expects of

him, nor will he work, as his father hopes; he will not even
bestow his society upon his dying benefactress during the last
few months of her life.   He has made his choice; he will go out
into the wide world with the beautiful Mrs. Wilton, who is the
personification of a not particularly high-flying type of the joy
of life.

In what a masterly way is this lady painted, and in how few
strokes of the brush; she who " is quite used to saying both ' yes '
and 'no' on her own account ! "   And what a delicate little touch it is
that whereas Ibsen introduces her to us as a lady " in the thirties "
—over thirty therefore—she herself, on the one occasion on which
she mentions her age, says to Erhart's mother, " Again and again
I've reminded him that I am seven years older than he "—that is
to say, than the youth of twenty-three !   She forgets a few years.
Finally, we have all her practical wisdom in the speech in which
she explains to the mother, half in jest, that she is taking little
Frida Foldal with her in case of accidents : " When Erhart is done
with me—and I with him—then it will be well for us both that
he, poor fellow, should have some one to fall back upon. . . .
I shall manage well enough for myself, I assure you."   It would
be impossible to portray a character more fully in a whole novel
than is done here in half a score of short speeches.

And every single one of the personages who appear in this
play is modelled for all time with the same monumental strength.

The construction of the drama is beyond all praise.   It rises
to its height of four stories as if built of iron on a foundation of
granite, firm and strong, clear and simple.   From beginning to
end it is instinct with feeling; there is intensity of feeling in the
kingdom of humbled self-righteousness in the lowest story, and
intensity of feeling in the shadow-kingdom above; in the end it is
the open-air feeling that prevails, and under its sway the man who
has so long been a captive draws his last breath.   The dramatic
storm-blast sweeps through the play.   The pulse of the drama
beats as fast as if it were keeping time with the pulse of a young
poet.   There are only minutes between the four acts—only one
minute indeed—so youthful is the impetus of the action.

But the spirit of the play reveals sufficiently that its author is
no longer a young man.   It is the spirit of wisdom—of stern
wisdom and radiant gentleness.   Its upshot is a great forbearance
towards human failings, which harmonises perfectly with severe

condemnation of hardness of heart—a deep compassion without any relaxation of moral fibre.

The Master-Builder, Little Eyolf, and *John Gabriel Borkman* are the first dramas that Ibsen, after a voluntary exile of nearly a generation, has written on Norwegian soil. He returned to Norway in 1891, and since then has lived in his native land. If in his young days he met with scant appreciation from his own people, now, in his later years, he is admired and idolised by the Norwegians as their chief title to world-wide renown.

Scandinavian literature is a different thing now from what it was at the time when he made a name with *Brand*, or when he opened up new paths with his dramas of modern life. In Norway as well as in Denmark, Iceland, Sweden, and Finland, a young literature has burst into blossom, rich in fresh talent, great and small. Each of the Scandinavian countries has led the way in turn, and at the present time they are all engaged in a vigorous, promising rivalry. Nevertheless there can scarcely be a doubt that Scandinavian literature has produced its best in Ibsen's dramas ; by them the outside world can measure the height it has attained, where it has built highest.

BJÖRNSTJERNE   BJÖRNSON

AUTHORISED TRANSLATION

By MARY MORISON

INTRODUCTORY NOTE

*The following Essay on Björnstjerne Björnson appeared,
along with the second of the foregoing "Impressions" of
Henrik Ibsen, in Dr. Brandes's "Moderne Gjennembruds-
mænd" (Pioneers of Modern Thought) in the year 1883.
It does not, therefore, present or attempt the complete
intellectual portraiture of Björnson which is embodied in
the three Essays on Ibsen. It is worth noting, however,
that a study of Björnson which stops short at the year 1882,
is not by any means so incomplete as a study of Ibsen
would be which should break off at the same date.
Björnson has done interesting and admirable work, especially in fiction, since 1882, but he has not, like Ibsen,
developed what may almost be called a new art. Politics
and social questions have to a considerable extent distracted
him from the pursuit of pure literature, and though the
past seventeen years will be of the highest importance to his
biographer, in considering him as a historical personality,
they will be less interesting to the student of literature,
who regards him primarily as a poet and a creative artist.
Therefore the disproportion between Dr. Brandes's treatment of Ibsen in the present volume, and his treatment of
Björnson, is not in reality so great as it may at first sight
appear.*

W. A.

BJÖRNSTJERNE BJÖRNSON

(1882)

IN the course of his speech on the occasion of the unveiling of
the statue of Wergeland, on 17th May 1881, Björnson said—

"No doubt you have all heard how, at one period of his life,
Henrik Wergeland went about with his pockets full of tree-seed,
and scattered a handful here and a handful there on his walks,
and tried to get his companions to do the same, ' because there
was no telling how much of it might come up.' This in itself is
a simple, touching, patriotism-breathing poem, worthy to rank
with the best he has written."

What Björnson here tells of Wergeland may be applied in
a higher sense to himself. He is Norway's great sower. The
land is a rocky land, bare and uncultivated. Much seed falls on
stony ground and is blown away by the wind; but the soil, where
there is soil, is receptive, the seed is sown plentifully, and
Björnson continues his task unweariedly. Much that he has
sown has already come up, and it is not of the present generation
alone that he thinks as he works.

The introductory chapter to *Arne*, which at the same time
forms the introductory chapter to the complete edition of
Björnson's novels, contains, as is well known, the fable of the
trees and the heather who determine to clothe the bare mountain
in front of them. Not aimlessly did Björnson disturb the
chronological order of his tales to place this chapter in the van.
It expresses the great idea of his life, the determination to
improve, to civilise his country by every means in his power.
This determination explains why he, the writer of such refined
and exquisite poetry, thinks it no degradation to do the rough

work of a journalist or popular orator, when there is any chance of advancing the moral or political education of the Norwegian people by combating some prejudice or error, propagating some simple, hitherto unacknowledged truth—or what he takes to be such. He has never regarded himself as simply a poet; he early accepted a wider vocation.

I

ONE only needs to look at Björnson to see how splendidly nature has equipped him for· the hard struggle which the literary life as a rule is. Seldom does one see such a powerful figure; it looks as if it were intended to be carved in granite. There is perhaps no other work which arouses every faculty to activity, excites the senses, refines and weakens the nervous system, in the same degree as the work of the author. But in Björnson's case there was no danger that the severe exertion of poetic production would affect the lungs, as it did in the case of Schiller and Keats, or the back, as in Heine's case; no danger that hostile newspaper articles would kill him, as they did his Halfdan in *The Editor*. There was nothing wrong with the marrow of that backbone, no dust or cough in those lungs; those shoulders were made to bear the blows the world gives, and to give hard ones back. And as to nerves! If Björnson has ever known from personal experience the meaning of what we call nerves— and it is quite probable that he has, for not with impunity is one the child of one's century—he certainly shows no trace of it in his writing; not when he is fastidiously refined, not even when, as at times, he is sentimental. He has none of that over-refinement which accompanies a slight degree of ill-health or exhaustion.

Strong as that beast of prey whose name occurs twice in his, we see him in our mind's eye, with the massive head, the close-shut mouth, and the piercing glance from behind the spectacles. His general appearance proclaims the pastor's son; his voice, play of feature, and gesticulation indicate more of the actor's talent than a poet usually possesses. No literary hostility could possibly crush him; and as to the greatest danger that threatens an author, the oblivion into which his name may chance to fall— a danger which for some years threatened his great rival, Henrik Ibsen—there could be no question of that with Björnson. As a young dramatic critic and politician, his literary *début* was so

I

bellicose as to excite much and noisy criticism. Like Thorbjörn in *Synnöve Solbakken*, he had in his early youth the propensity to fight which goes along with strength; like Sigurd in *Sigurd's Flight*, he fought, in the first instance to try his strength, in the second from a simple and strong, if often mistaken, sense of right. In any case, he thoroughly understood the art of drawing attention to himself.

This is as much as to say that he, with his sanguine, sunny disposition, felt himself in his element in the broad daylight of life. He had none of that dread of the light which so frequently forms a trait in the temperament or character of shyer or more reserved men, who have always something to overcome when they make public display of their physical or mental individuality. Ibsen has described this feeling in his poem *A Shunner of the Daylight* :—

"No longer night and its goblins
    Strike terror to my heart;
'Tis the sights and sounds of daylight
    That make me shiver and start.

Under the black wings of darkness
    I take my refuge now,
There cherish my old-time longings,
    Face fate with undaunted brow.

But bared of night's thick covering,
    Counsel nor strength I find—
'Twill be a deed of darkness
    That calls my name to mind."[1]

---

[1] "Nu er det Dagens Trolde
    nu er det Livets Larm
    der drysser alle de kolde
    Rædsler i min Barm.

Jeg gjemmer mig under Fligen
    af Mörkets Skræmselsslör,
    da ruster sig al min Higen
    saa örnedjærv som för.

Dog fattes mig Nattens Foerværk,
    jeg ved ej mit arme Raad,
    ja över jeg engang et Storværk,
    saa blir det en Mörkets Daad."

No nature could be more unlike Björnson's than that which describes itself in these beautiful, brave words, which seem to point towards *A Doll's House* and *Ghosts.*

By nature Björnson is half chieftain, half poet, combining in his personality these two most striking figures of ancient Norway, the chief and the skald. By turn of thought he is half tribune, half lay-preacher, his public utterances being distinguished by a combination of the political and the religious earnestness of his countrymen, and this in a more marked degree after than before his secession from orthodoxy. Since his apostasy he has been more markedly the missionary, the reformer. Before that it often seemed as if his ego were of more importance to him than all else, whereas now the ego is absorbed in the cause.

An author may possess great and rare gifts, and yet be long prevented from making his way, either by his genius being apparently out of harmony with the character of his nation, or by its being really out of harmony with the actual stage of that nation's development. Many of the greatest have thus suffered. Many, among them Byron, Heine, Henrik Ibsen, have forsaken their country; many more, who have remained, have felt themselves forsaken by their countrymen. Björnson's experience has been a very different one. He has never, indeed, been unanimously accepted by the whole Norwegian nation—at first because his style was so new, afterwards because his ideas were so defiantly daring—but yet he has his whole nation with him and at his back, as no other living poet has, except perhaps Victor Hugo. And Hugo is not so French as Björnson is Norwegian. To name the name of Björnson is like hoisting the Norwegian flag. In his merits and his faults, his genius and his weakness, he is as distinctively national as Voltaire or Schiller. It might seem as if Ibsen, with his shyness and peculiarity, his seriousness and reserve, were more typically national than Björnson, the bright herald of the future. But the Norwegian poets of the eighteenth century and Wergeland sufficiently proved that open-heartedness, freedom and loudness of speech, buoyancy and vivacity, also are Norwegian; and in Björnson's art, in the creatures of his imagination, we have the taciturnity, the reticence, the shyness, the ponderousness. Free-spoken as a man, laconic as an artist, touchily patriotic, and at the same time vividly conscious of his nation's narrow-mindedness, its spiritual poverty and needs—a consciousness that has impelled him to Scandinavism, Teutonism, cosmopolitanism—this peculiar mingling of qualities is so typically national that Björnson in his own person comprehends the nation. He represents its self-criticism—not a criticism that chastises with scorpions, like Turgueneff's or Ibsen's, but a severe, courageous judgment, inspired by love, pronounced without sadness. For he never lays bare a weakness in the correction and ultimate cure of which he does not believe, nor a vice of whose eradication he despairs. He has an implicit faith in the goodness of human nature, along with the unconquerable optimism of the pronounced sanguine temperament.

No other country could have produced him, and it would have been less possible for him than for other artists to thrive in any country but his own. In 1880, when a report was spread in the German newspapers that he intended to take up his residence in Munich because he was tired of the strife at home, he wrote in a private letter: " I will live in Norway; I will thrash and be thrashed in Norway; I will sing and die in Norway—of that you may be certain ! "

It is a great thing for a man to feel himself thus bound up with his nation, if he is at the same time sympathetically understood by it; and this Björnson is, by reason of the fundamental qualities of his nature. An enthusiastic admirer of the reserved and solitary Michael Angelo, he is himself a character of a totally different type—not solitary even when he is in the completest solitude (as he has been since 1873 on his property in Gausdal), but a thoroughly social and popular character. He admires Michael Angelo because he admires greatness, earnestness, sad severity in the human soul and in art; but he has nothing in common with the great Florentine's solitariness. He is the born party-founder, and he early felt himself attracted by such eager, popular party-founders as Wergeland and Grundtvig, unlike as he is to both in his plastic, constructive power. It is a necessity to him to feel himself a central point or focus of sympathies, and he involuntarily collects a party round him, because he is himself a society and party mirror.

That he is typically national is further to be ascribed to the fact that he is a popular spirit, a spiritual representative of the people. This, too, was predetermined by his nature. He is popular because he is not reserved and not ultra-refined, because, to begin with, there was something rough-hewn about him, something that showed kinship with the many.   There are characters who begin their career by speaking in the name of the many, and there are others who, till the day of their death, speak only in their own name; there are characters who from the beginning say "we," others who from first to last say "I," and others, again, who begin by saying "I" and end by saying "we."   Björnson, in spite of his great independence, has ever felt himself to be an organ, has felt as if a whole people made its voice heard through his.   He has felt himself, as it were, borne onwards by his country, its past history, its present aims, and in the strength of this feeling he has spoken.

All minds of this type have one feature in common: they have no repugnance to general, accepted truths.   However new and original the form in which they present it, the matter represented is, to begin with, something universally accepted and recognised.   The very constitution of these minds precludes any distaste for general religious, moral, and political truths; and it is to this bond with ordinary humanity that they, in the first instance, owe their influence and their success.   Minds like Kierkegaard's in the domain of religion, Ibsen's in that of morals, Andræ's in politics, doubt the trustworthiness of universally accepted truths from the very fact of their being such.   The exact opposite is the case with Björnson; even in his hottest struggle with convention, he fights in the name of the great majority.

To this he owes his health of mind; herein lies his strength. In the possession of too aristocratic sensibilities, too high a degree of mental refinement, too intense a hatred of conventionalities, lies a danger for the author.   Nervous sensibility is not conducive to popularity.   What is far-fetched, cautious, difficult of apprehension, is despised or overlooked by the masses. They demand of the popular orator a powerful voice, a broad sense of humour, clear, simple thoughts graphically expressed; and of the popular poet a beautiful, glorified reproduction of their characteristics and of their own simple form of art.   Everything of this nature that a nation could demand, Björnson has abundantly supplied.

II

BJÖRNSTJERNE BJÖRNSON was born on the 8th of December
1832, in one of the valleys of the Dovrefjeld, at Kvikne, where
his father was pastor. In this district nature is bleak and barren;
the mountains are bare; fir and birch grow here and there, but
both soil and climate are so bad that the peasant can only
reckon on one grain harvest in five years. Nothing would thrive
on the pastor's farm. In the scantily populated valley the houses
lay far apart. In winter snow covered everything, formed a high
embankment round each house, and offered abundant opportunity
for sledging and snow-shoeing.

When little Björnstjerne was six years old, his father was
appointed to Næs, in the Romsdal, one of the most beautiful
districts in Norway. On both sides of the valley rise mountains
with wild, bold peaks, which take more and more singular forms
as the valley descends and approaches the fjord.

> " Peak above peak to view appearing,
>   The loins of the one at the other's shoulder,
>   Their giant heads 'gainst heaven rearing,
>   Higher they mount and ever bolder.
>   We stand and wait some crash infernal :
>   More awful is the silence eternal.
>
>   Many are white-clad, many are blue,
>   With pinnacles pointed, straining, fire-lighted ;
>   In long chains united
>   Others press forward like brothers true." [1]

---

[1] " Hvor vidt jeg ogsaa lar Öjet vandre,
        den ene Bærg-Kjæmpe over den andre,
        den enes Lænd ved den andens Skulder
        og dette til yderste Himmel-Brynet.
        Man staar og venter et Verdens-Bulder :
        den evige Stilhed forstörrer Synet.

        Somme staar hvide, somme staar blaa
        med takkede, kappende, hidsige Tinder,
        somme sig binder
        sammen i Kjæder og fremad gaa."

Few Norwegian valleys can compare in rich variety with the Romsdal. The district is a fertile one, comparatively thickly populated; the pretty farm-houses are mostly two-storeyed; the inhabitants, though laconic in speech, are frank, vivacious and capricious, passionate and changeable, as if influenced by the "squall-fjords" in whose neighbourhood they live. The striking difference between this home and the last was not without its effect on the child; it taught him to reflect and compare; to look at himself with new eyes, and to become conscious of his individuality. The grand scenery and the stir of life filled the boy's receptive mind with pictures. When he was sent to the grammar-school in the little town of Molde, he organised unions among the boys, and soon became a kind of leader among them. He already read everything he could get hold of in the way of history and poetry. From popular fairy-tales like Asbjörnsen's, and popular songs, such as those which Landstad had lately collected, he acquired the impression of the people conveyed by the romanticism of the period; but along with these he read the sagas and devoured the writings of Wergeland. At the age of seventeen he went to Christiania to prepare for his matriculation. There he devoted much of his time to the study of Danish literature, became the friend of Aasmund Vinje and Ernst Sars, and led the stirring life of a high-spirited youth. The Danish theatre in Christiania, at that time under very careful management, interested and influenced him. He returned home in 1852, and during the year that he spent there, the life of the people showed itself to him in a new and still more attractive light, and he began to write songs in the popular style, which the peasants sang.

After his return to Christiania he brought himself into notice chiefly as a critic. He wrote with all the usual impetuosity of gifted youth, added to all the prejudices of the budding poet, and made many enemies. The writings of the Danish thinkers of the literary period which had just come to a close—Heiberg, Sibbern, Kierkegaard—formed his principal study at this time, and somewhat later he began to be absorbed in Grundtvig's emotionalism. The insistence of Grundtvigianism on the lawfulness of the joy of life, as opposed to the gloom of Norwegian pietism, and also its strong faith in the genius and mission of Scandinavia, had an irresistible attraction for a characteristically Scandinavian youth who had little acquaintance with the rest of Europe. Grundtvig's influence upon him makes itself felt until far on in the seventies. The child from the lonely parsonage, the schoolboy from the unimportant little town, the student of a university whose professors were able men, but not in touch with the rest of Europe, found at that period in Grundtvigianism what he has always sought, but has since found without its pale—the highest, freest human development.

A visit to Sweden on the occasion of the Scandinavian students' festival at Upsala in 1856, and, shortly after that, a longer stay in Copenhagen, served to ripen Björnson's productive faculty. After making a first sketch of *Married*, which he was unable at that time to complete, he wrote his first dramatic work, the little play *Between the Battles*. The simple, brusque prose of this piece formed a striking contrast to the wordy pathos of the Oehlenschläger school. It was rejected by Heiberg as director of the Theatre Royal of Copenhagen, was acted in Christiania, and subsequently printed. How much further Björnson, and later literature generally, have travelled in the direction then taken, can be best judged by re-reading this little play, which on its appearance repelled by what was then considered savagery of subject and harshness of treatment, whereas now it seems to us quite idyllic and much too sentimental.

For some time Björnson had felt a growing impulse to write stories of peasant life. The experiences and reading of his early youth led him "to see the peasant in the light of the sagas, and the sagas in the light of the peasant." *Synnöve Solbakken*, *A Father*, *The Eagle's Nest*, revivified the saga style. And this style, created in its graphic simplicity in olden days for the narration of tales of manslaughter, feud, incendiarism, wild and marvellous adventure, now elevated by its grandeur the idyllic theme of the loves of the young Norwegian peasantry.

Björnson belongs to those lucky writers who find their style at once. *Synnöve Solbakken*, his first tale, is like a flawless cast. He had no hard struggle with an unmanageable material before he succeeded in giving his works their inward equilibrium. They flowed from the melting-pot into the mould, and stood before us in clear contour and monumental solidity.

This does not mean that Björnson as an author has been exempted from all necessity to feel his way, to alter his course. But his career has not been, like that of so many others, an ascent in the mist, with a few hours of sunshine on the mountain-top. It has been an ascent in fair weather, with many a clear and beautiful view. To speak more plainly, his development has been this: Beginning with few and narrow ideas, he neverthe-less began with the perfection of the accomplished artist, and as time went on he endowed his works with his own ever-increasing supply of ideas and ever more accurate knowledge of the human heart. In the course of this progress he may have lost nothing as far as creative ability is concerned, but he has certainly lost in the matter of form, of classic balance.

Björnson's first works were not received with unanimous enthusiasm. His earliest tales and dramas were so exactly the opposite of what the public were accustomed to admire, that they could not but arouse hostile criticism. Many of the cultivated literary class, wedded to the older style, inevitably felt their æsthetic creed attacked. The melodious tones of Oehlenschläger's sonorous sentiment still rang in every one's ears, and to men of the old school his representation of ancient and mediæval Norway, though externally less correct, seemed to convey more inward conviction than Björnson's; Henrik Hertz's unsurpassed refinement and charm of style had weakened men's appreciation of broad strength; and, finally, in this new Norwegian literature the reading public missed that high degree of philosophic culture which Heiberg had accustomed them to look for and find in the poet. I still distinctly remember what strange productions *Synnöve Solbakken* and *Arne* seemed to me on their first appearance.

Björnson's literary reputation was nevertheless speedily estab-lished, and perhaps nothing contributed more to this than the fact that the ruling party in Denmark, the Scandinavian and National-Liberal party, took this new literary development under its protection. At that time the National-Liberals in Denmark and the Scandinavians in Norway were still in literature the friends of the peasant. They loved the abstract, without know-ing much about the real, concrete peasant. They had given him the franchise, feeling convinced that for ages to come he would allow himself to be led by those who had given him "freedom," in the hope that he would make use of his "freedom" only to elect and obey them and their like. Therefore they still saw in him the sound core of the nation, the descendant of the mighty

men of old, and they flattered him and made him a hero of
romance.   Hence works which delicately, tactfully, and in a new
and grand literary style glorified peasant life, were sure of a good
reception in Denmark, especially coming as they did from one
of those "brother countries" which lay almost nearer to the
true Scandinavian Dane's heart than his own.

In addition to this, Björnson's representations of peasant life
had the same attraction for the *blasé* Copenhagener that written
or acted pastoral plays had for the eighteenth-century courtier.
People were too critical now to want high-heeled shepherdesses
leading lambs with silk ribbons round their necks; but they
found a substitute for this sort of thing in the Norwegian youths
and maidens whose feelings were as delicate and deep as those
of any educated gentleman or lady.

The peasant novel in itself was not a new literary departure.
Steen Steensen Blicher had introduced it in the beginning of the
thirties with his excellent pictures of Jutland peasant life.   In
1839 Immermann, in the masterly tale *Der Oberhof* (incorporated
in his larger work *Münchhausen*), half unconsciously established
it as a form of literary art.   In 1843 Auerbach published the
Schwarzwalder Dorfgeschichten, and it was under his treatment
that the village romance became a distinct literary species; this
was the first time that a German author had devoted himself to
the study of the characters and events of the quiet village.
When George Sand, who was brought up in the country, and
retired to the country again at the close of her stormily romantic
youth, heard of Auerbach's novels, she felt the inclination to try
a similar experiment, and in *Jeanne* (1844), *François le Champi*,
La Mare au Diable, &c., she presented France with a series of
delicately idealistic rural tales.

It is said that Björnson, at the time he began to produce his
peasant stories, had no acquaintance with the writings of Auerbach and his followers.   In any case he had little in common
with Auerbach.   The Norwegian peasant romance differs from
the German in two of its characteristics.   Auerbach's works are
epics, which delineate the peasant's life in its entirety.   We see
him at his daily work in the field and the farmyard; we learn
to understand his ways—his slowness, his subjection to the
power of habit and custom.   In Björnson's writings all this detail
is condensed, brief, and only occurs for the sake of the love-

story. Secondly, Auerbach's village tales are written from a point of view which is not that of the peasant, not that of his heroes and heroines. He did not incorporate in them the feelings, the faith of his childhood. He was the scholar and the philosopher, the representative of all the rich and many-sided mental culture of the day. He had been a personal disciple of Schelling; he had made his *début* with a novel which had for its hero Spinoza, a philosopher whose works he translated into German, and whose views he early assimilated, and continued all his life long to proclaim. He certainly remoulded his master's philosophy to suit his own needs and sympathies—it is very doubtful if Spinoza would have taken any interest in those finite beings, those limited intelligences, whom we know by the name of peasants. He interpreted Spinoza's philosophy as the gospel of nature, proclaimed him to be the apostle of natural religion and natural piety. Auerbach loved to portray peasants, because to him they were a piece of nature; he loved to search in these undeveloped minds for the germs of that philosophy of life which he considered to be the true, the inevitably victorious one. His classical tale, *Barfüssele*, opposes to the orthodox ethical code that of the young, barefooted peasant girl with the strong instinct of acquisition, who, in defiance of the Scriptural command to turn our left cheek to him who smites us on the right, goes through life with clenched fists, submits to no injustice, and yet meets with no consequent humiliation. The tone of these books bears the impress of the impassioned political feeling of the forties in Germany, of the vehement desire to elevate the working-man to the comprehension of the educated man's ideals in religion and politics. In Björnson's tales of peasant life the relation of the author to his subject is a perfectly different one. In all essentials his view of life is the same as that of his heroes; he does not write as the disciple of any school of philosophy. It is not the superior mind, but the gifted poet and artist, who meets the reader in these pages. Hence their limitations, but hence also the wonderful unity of style and tone.

Literature was the gainer. The softest emotions were expressed in the severest of forms. The soul of these works was a lyric fervour, which penetrated everywhere, and found its freest outlet in the numerous songs scattered throughout them—children's songs, love songs, patriotic songs. The keynote of romance re-

sounded through them all. It did not seem the least unnatural
that the tale should, as in the case of *Arne*, be introduced by a
fable; and in spite of the stern realism of some of the character-
drawing, the general effect was so idyllic, that the small stories
interspersed here and there, in which fairies played a part, were
quite in keeping with the spirit of the whole. The author was a
good observer; like his own Arne he had the gift of retaining
scenes and impressions which others allowed to escape from
their memories, and thus his observation provided him with a
store of realistic details. But apart from this, popular song and
legend were the two fountains the mingling of whose waters
formed the crystal of his art. It was not an art which he created
in solitary greatness; through it he was in countless ways in
touch with the mind of the people.

Synnöve is plastic harmony within the limits of Norwegian
peasant life, and its hero, Thorbjörn, the type of the strong,
fierce youth who must be subdued and softened before he can
find rest. *Arne*, on the contrary, is the longing to overstep these
limits and be off, "over the hills and far away;" the lyric,
imaginative propensity in the national character; the Viking
instinct transformed into a longing for travel; and its hero is the
type of the soft, dreamy youth who must be hardened before
he can become a man. *A Happy Boy* is a fresh breeze blowing
upon the oppressive heaviness that weighs down the Norwegian
temperament, a glad message of courage and joy, a fresh
laughing-song that clears the air.

III

DRAMAS and poems followed. The great personality gradually shook itself free from the trammels of popularity. In *Between the Battles, Sigurd Slembe, Arnljot Gelline,* everywhere we meet the same heroic type, the born chief and benefactor of his people, whose rights are withheld from him, and who is forced by the injustice he suffers to do much evil in the struggle towards his goal. In *Between the Battles* Sverre himself laments that he leaves towns in flames behind him wherever he goes. Sigurd's desire is the good of Norway, yet he is hated and hunted down, because, kept from the throne which is his by right, he has become "a king in the panoply of revenge, with the glance of despair, and a sword of flame." Arnljot, at heart so loving and so humble, becomes a robber and incendiary, who plunders, burns, and murders, until he meets his death fighting for Olaf at Stiklestad.

These characters are rooted deep in their author's own nature. He himself early became "a sign to be spoken against." With his unbounded ambition, his impetuous nature, his kindness of heart, he felt himself akin to these saga heroes. His desire was to elevate and unite his people, and to be one with them; and this craving and the feeling of the occasional discord between him and them, the feeling that he was at times misunderstood and scorned, he embodied in these old chiefs—in that Sigurd who, when angered, became "hard as steel," yet whose heart was full to overflowing of plans for his people's welfare.

There is a record of much silent endurance on Björnson's part in that monologue of Sigurd's in the second last scene of the play, which begins: "The Danes forsake me? The battle lost? Thus far and no farther?"—in which plans for raising an army, crossing the sea, becoming a merchant, a crusader, suggest themselves and are rejected, until the words "Thus far and no farther" recur again as a terrible refrain, as apprehension of utter ruin—not question this time, but answer. Yet love of his country speaks even from the depths of Sigurd's despair—of that country for which he longed when far away, as children long for Christmas, though he had dealt it blow upon blow. The great personality Björnson has nothing of the solitary grandeur of the great personality Michael Angelo. The popular is his element; when he leaves it, it is only to long to return to it; he would be one with his people, and suffers keenly when the desired union is frustrated.

Ibsen's is a solitary nature; he is "lonely, far removed." He descends into the depths like the miner.

> "Break the way, thou hammer pond'rous,
> To the secret chambers wondrous."[1]

Björnson's nature does not incline downwards, but outwards; his genius is open-armed.

Another contrast between the two poets may be noticed in connection with this one and with the Northern dramas, viz., their different attitude towards nature. The born dramatist, Ibsen, is not given to description of nature; it has no attraction for him; in his loneliness of mind he shuts himself off from nature as he does from human beings. In his youth his principal characters were often personifications of an idea, with the want of substance of imaginary beings. Even when he introduces nature with powerful effect, as in the case of the ice-church in *Brand*, it is more as symbol than as reality. Björnson's mind, less circumscribed, loves to dwell on the characteristic features of Northern nature, and communicates an impression of them even in drama. The scene between Sigurd and the Finn maiden, one of the most beautiful he has written, is an example of this. Where she comes suddenly on the scene with her dogs she brings the whole of Northern nature in her train. She appears in a gleam of the aurora borealis, and the luminous magic of the midnight sun is felt in her words; her happy love of life, of the sun, of the summer, her unreturned love for Sigurd, the delicate and ephemeral nature of her grief—the whole is a living poem of nature; and this is felt by Sigurd. For Björnson has given to all his ancient Norsemen his own modern love of nature. Think,

[1] "Bryd mig Vejen, tunge Hammer,
til det Dulgtes Hjertekammer."

for instance, of *Arnljot's Longing for the Sea*, in the rhythm of which we hear the sea's monotonous rise and fall :—

> "The full moon draweth, the storm upheaveth,
> Their grip relaxeth, the tide wide streameth." [1]

Others have painted the sea in its uncontrollableness and pitilessness ; Björnson paints its cold brow caressed by the sun, its chilling calm, its profound melancholy, and makes us hear the lullaby of death in its monotonous murmur.   And Arnljot's words when he tells how, after he is dead, the waves "will roll his name shorewards on clear moonlight nights," are so characteristic that they may well come to be applied to the poet himself.   A hundred years hence, lovers looking from the shore at the great waves rolling in under the light of the moon, will remember Björnson's name.

[1] "Fuldmaanen suger, Orkanen löfter,
     men Taget glipper, og Vandet strömmer."

IV

BJÖRNSON has twice been theatrical manager, 1857–59 in Bergen, 1865–67 in Christiania. In the autumn of 1857, on the invitation of Ole Bull, he undertook the management of the theatre of the lively provincial town. He brought it into a flourishing condition, and spent two happy years in the companionship of Ole Bull, to whom he afterwards dedicated *Arne*. As director of the Christiania theatre he exercised a beneficial but too short-lived influence. He possesses so many of the qualities of a good actor that he makes an excellent stage-manager. If he had previously done his best to drive Danish theatrical art out of Norway, he now made up for it by doing his best to found a national stage. The pity is that he did not continue to build on the foundation that he laid; it has been a loss to the Norwegian theatre and to himself. His experiences as a theatrical manager have naturally been of value to him as a dramatic author; but in this latter capacity he has never attained to technical perfection, probably for the very reason that there has been no continuous interchange of influence between the theatre and him. His grand and beautiful trilogy, *Sigurd Slembe*, was not written for the stage, and as yet has only been played by the Meiningen company, never in Scandinavia. It contains some powerfully dramatic scenes, those, for instance, which follow directly on the murder of the king, but the play taken as a whole is a reading-play. His strong and stormily passionate youthful work, *Halting Hulda*, gains little by representation. But two plays of his first period, *Maria Stuart* (1864) and *Married* (1865), have been remarkably successful on the stage.

Maria Stuart is a luxuriant and powerful production, welling over with dramatic life, but as noisily stagey as a melodrama. The acts end in true catastrophes; the concluding scenes of the second and third acts are genuinely dramatic in their violence and the feeling of excited expectancy they arouse; but the play ends weakly, or, to speak more correctly, does not end at all. All

the details of the action—the assassination of Rizzio, the murder
of Darnley, Bothwell's abduction of Mary—fit into each other,
and produce the effect of logical consequences; a gust of stormy
youthfulness sweeps through the whole.

The poet's great success in the treatment of this subject is
probably due to the fact that on Scottish ground he still felt
himself in Norwegian air. Bothwell says: "From the moment
that my will struck root in the soil of events and circumstances,
I have seen it grow above them, with a blood-red stem, but with
mighty branches. The Norwegian Viking race from which we
claim descent was one of these will-trees; it was driven on these
shores, it struck root in their rocks, and now the people dwell
beneath its shade." In this Norwegian-Scottish world the poet
feels himself completely at home, and, without any weakening of
the local colouring, he gave his characters traits that showed
kinship with the mediæval Norwegian types he was accustomed
to portray. He was successful, too, in his presentation of Puri-
tanism. There was no corresponding phenomenon in the Norway
of those old days, but he could study one much nearer his own
time. For although Christianity had been nominally introduced
into Norway nine hundred years before, it was practically introduced by Hans Nilsen Hauge in the beginning of the nineteenth
century. In the light of Haugianism and pietism Björnson understood John Knox. His other notably successful characters were
Bothwell and Darnley. The former is a genuine Renaissance
type; the latter, in his boyish vindictiveness and undignified
humility, is almost modern. Mary Stuart herself is not quite so
successfully drawn; there is something too intangible about her.
She is a being the mysterious depths of whose nature are revealed
to us in contradictory manifestations—she is her sex in its
strength and in its weakness. Her fate is to a certain extent
determined by her nature, whose weakness is the measure of her
power over men, whose strength is powerless under the conditions
of these wild and lawless times. There is too much Northern
idealism in this character delineation. I do not exactly mean by
this that Björnson's Mary Stuart is too pure, though I believe
that she is. The historic Mary Stuart was not the sphinx of
sensuality, cruelty, and coldness whom we meet in the pages of
Swinburne's *Chastelard*, yet Swinburne probably came nearer to
historic truth than Björnson. There is nothing dæmonic in

K

Björnson's Mary, and little that recalls the Renaissance period. His conception of her is moreover conveyed to us less by what she says or does herself than by means of enthusiastic praise or disparaging mention on the part of others, and by the remarkable effects produced by the exercise of her direct personal charm, a kind of magic spell the nature of which is not made clear to the audience. She stands as it were in a cloud of adjectival definitions hurled in her direction by the other personages of the drama. *Maria Stuart* dates from a period in Björnson's development when (perhaps under the influence of Kierkegaard) he was inclined to give psychological descriptions of his characters instead of allowing them to display their own natures without commentary. All the personages in this drama are psychologists, who study one another, discuss one another's characters, and experiment on one another. Even William Taylor, the page, understands and describes Darnley's mental condition as a doctor understands and describes the state of a patient. Murray and Darnley describe each other; Lethington describes Bothwell and Murray; Mary seeks the key to Rizzio's, Knox the key to Darnley's character; the murder of Rizzio itself, considered carefully, is a psychological experiment which Darnley tries on Mary, thinking to win her back by fear, as he has failed to do it by love. These people may all think like psychologists, but they all speak like poets, and the splendour of this poetic, almost Shakespearian language, which is yet perfectly natural—for the men of the Renaissance as a rule felt like artists and expressed themselves like poets— heightens the effect produced on us by the profound originality of the principal characters.

The subject of the little play *Married* is a simple, everyday event in human life—the separation of the young bride from her parents' home, the struggle in her soul between the inborn, firmly established love to father and mother, and the new, still feeble love to her husband—a revolution or evolution which takes place with the natural necessity and suffering of a spiritual birth. In ordinary circumstances this break in a woman's life does not stand out so sharply, because it is accepted as something inevitable, and because it not unfrequently has more the character of a deliverance than of a rupture. But let the circumstances be conceived as somewhat less normal, let the parents' affection be unusually egotistical or unusually tender, and the well-brought-up daughter's love to the man of her choice much less strongly developed than her filial affection, and we at once have a problem, a dramatic collision, a conflict with an uncertain issue. The idea is a simple and excellent one.

Several faults may be found with the execution. To begin with the chief: How can Axel, who has had the greatest difficulty in persuading Laura to tear herself away from her home, be weak and stupid enough to allow that home, in the person of Mathilde, to follow her on their journey? Without her everything would have gone more smoothly and easily. We are certainly told at the end of the play that without her the two would never have found each other; but this is not self-evident, and in any case it is an unfortunate complication. The author's aim should rather have been to show how the two became truly one without extraneous help; it is a clumsy expedient to make a *dea ex machina* write an anonymous novel, with a description of the couple's own situation which so alarms them that it drives them into each other's arms. In this device I see a sign of the times in which the play was written. The air was full of Kierkegaard's theories. The application of scientific observation and experiment in the domain of human intercourse, that experimental psychology which plays so important a part in Kierkegaard's philosophy, and was so conspicuous in *Maria Stuart*, presents itself to us in *Married* in the person of Mathilde, the friend of the family. And the whole treatment of love and passion throughout the play is characteristic of that period of Björnson's and of Scandinavian mental development. Little interest was taken in instincts and propensities for their own sake; they were studied and delineated in their relation to ethics and positive religion. The poetical representation of love before marriage, or outside the bonds of wedlock, was looked upon as frivolous or immoral; the demand was for the poetry of marriage, which Kierkegaard in his *Either, Or*, had proclaimed to be a far nobler species. In the course of the poet's endeavours to satisfy the widespread craving for morality, it occasionally happened that the passion to be legalised shrank into nothing, like the sugar in the paws of the washing-bear. The germ of love which is fostered in *Married* is so weak and sapless that it is hardly worth all the care and toil that are lavished on it. Love is represented throughout to the wife as the duty she owes to her husband, is kept before her

eyes as a task, a claim.   It is no wild, free-growing plant of nature;
it comes to maturity in the hot-house of duty, hedged round
by Axel's tenderness, forced on by the artificial fire of jealousy,
anxiety, and fear of loss which Mathilde kindles.   There is an
old French song which runs—

> " Ah ! si l'amour prenait racine,
>   j'en planterais dans mon jardin,
>   j'en planterais, j'en semerais
>   aux quatre coins,
>   j'en donnerais aux amoureux
>   qui n'en ont point."

This verse has come into my mind every time I have seen
or read *Married*.   I adore Eros, the grand and beautiful ; but
I take no pleasure in seeing how little weakling Eroses are
brought up on the bottle.   My taste is not that of the public,
for no play has been more successful on the stage than this, or
has gone through more editions.

V

A SPECULATIVE Danish bookseller in the sixties published a calendar, for which he engaged well-known poets of the day to write short poems. Each was to choose his month. Björnson wrote the little poem of which the first verse is—

> " 'Tis April tunes my lyre !
> Then all that's old is falling,
> The new life loud is calling.
> Who heeds the storm and clatter ?
> Than peace there's something better—
> The ardour of desire." [1]

It is a characterisation of his own attitude during that first period. He felt a keen desire to play the part of reformer in every domain ; and in more than one he actually was a reformer, without a particularly clear idea of what he was aiming at. In none did he do such characteristic, remarkable, imperishable work as in the domain of lyric poetry, and this in spite of his being by no means a correct versifier. His popular ballads and songs have the genuine ring, his patriotic songs have become national songs, and in his one or two ancient Norwegian narratives or monologues he has caught the antique style in a way which Oehlenschläger and Tegnér never succeeded in doing.

As an example of his popular style, take the ballad of *Nils Finn*. It is a simple story of a little boy who loses his snow-shoes, and, drawn down by the earth-spirits, sinks into the snow and perishes. Lobedanz has aptly compared it to Goethe's *Erlkönig ;* and though it is in a different style—burlesque in its horror, where the other is pathetic—it undoubtedly stands the

[1] " Jeg vælger mig April !
i den det Gamle falder,
i den det Ny faar Fæste ;
det volder lidt Rabalder—
dog Fred er ej det bedste,
men at man Noget vil."

comparison. It has a humour which resembles the humour of
the Porter in *Macbeth*, and with all its simplicity it shows
powerful imagination. The horror of the incident is alleviated
by the comical ending, which reminds us of the way in which
terrible occurrences are communicated in legends and fairy
tales—

> " On the snow stood two shoes and looked round and round;
>   As nothing was there, there was nought to be found.
>   —'Where is Nils?' resounded the cry." [1]

One has only to read carefully a few lines of any of Björnson's
patriotic songs to understand their widespread popularity. The
most popular of all begins—

> " Yes, we love that land so rock-bound,
>   Rising from the foam ;
>   On its weather-beaten bosom
>   Many a thousand home." [2]

It would be impossible to convey more concisely and more perfectly the impression produced on a Norwegian by the sight of
his native land as he approaches it from the sea.

In *The Norwegian Students' Greeting to Welhaven* we have
a flawlessly perfect poem of a species not much cultivated by
Björnson, with an elaborate metre, strictly adhered to. It is to
be observed that the second and third stanzas of this poem,
in spite of all difficulties, ring as fresh and melodious as the
first. We know how rare this is, especially in the case of the
natural poet. There is certainly nothing like it to be found in
Wergeland.

Of Björnson's longer lyric pieces *Bergliot* is undoubtedly the
most remarkable. It is the lament of Bergliot, the widow of the
chieftain Ejnar Tambarskelve, for her murdered husband, and for

[1] " Tvau ski stod i snjoin og saa sig ikring
    men de saa inki stort ; fyr' der var Ingenting.
    —' Kvar er Nils?' sa d'uppundir."

[2] " Ja vi elsker dette Landet
    som det stiger frem
    furet, vejrbidt over Vandet
    med de tusind Hjem."

her only son, who lies dead by his side.   How simple and unlike
the stereotype tragedy-style is this wail—

> " I'll close the doors of our home so stately,
> Horses and cattle I will sell,
> I'll send away our men and maidens,
> Go forth myself and live alone."

Neither Oehlenschläger nor Hertz would have dared to let a
heroic female character introduce the sale of cows and horses
into her first outburst of grief.   I know nothing in any modern
treatment of an old Scandinavian theme which has made the
same impression on me as the refrain-like recurrence of Bergliot's
order to the servant who is driving the chariot on which she sits
with the corpses of her husband and her son—

> " Drive slowly ; thus drove Ejnar always
>   —We'll soon enough reach home." [1]

The words "thus drove Ejnar always" paint with admirable
simplicity the chief's dignity, the quiet majesty of his demeanour ;
the other clause, "we'll soon enough reach home," indicates, in
the fewest possible words, the emptiness and bitterness of the
life that awaits her.

[1] " Kjör langsomt ; thi saadan kjörte Ejnar altid
    —og vi kommer tidsnok hjem."

VI

BJÖRNSON attained this level early.

All the best works of his first period were written by the time he was a little over thirty, and people were already beginning to think of these works as of a completed series. No one could be blind to their remarkable qualities, but they showed no trace of proper development. Their author's productive power maintained itself for a long time at the same level; but his view of life became no wider; it remained childish and narrow. At times he could be commonplace; he occasionally wrote a poem that almost smacked of the schoolboy; and he gave expression to an absolutely childish optimism in such verses as *Then and Now* (fortunately not included in the second edition of his poems). He invoked the Almighty on the occasion of every wedding and every funeral, printed His actual words between inverted commas in the poem on Munch, introduced and took liberties with Him in every single verse that was intended to be impressively solemn. He sang of "the child in our soul"; maintained that we can conceive of nothing higher, nothing greater, than children and child-like souls; declared (in the poem to Sverdrup) that he took his stand on the faith of his childhood, and that it was from that standpoint he demanded equality and liberty for all. It was probably from the same standpoint that in the poem to Frederick the Seventh he designated that king "Denmark's warmest, greatest heart, his country's strongest fortress," &c., &c. Like almost all contemporary Scandinavian writers, he kept at a careful distance from the enlightened thought and life of the day. Or perhaps it would be more correct to say, that when he represented men and ideas of the day he did it unintentionally; they appeared dressed, disguised, in old Norwegian or mediæval Scottish theatrical costumes. In *Sigurd Slembe* we have Helga and Frakark discussing the relative theories of the immortality of the race and of the individual in terms which remind us too forcibly of 1862. And the chieftains who discuss politics as if they were acquainted with the history of the next seven centuries, who use such expressions as "a vocation," "an imperative mission," "the constitution," "to base the law on an illegal foundation," these same chieftains break the captive Sigurd on the wheel limb by limb—a proceeding which presupposes an entirely different grade of civilisation.   People who express themselves in such a cultivated manner do not break their enemies on the wheel, they slander them.

Added to this want of conformity between the characters' thoughts and their passions, we have the author's tendency, regretable from the artistic point of view, so to concentrate all his great scenes and characters in the course of the action that the orthodox faith may envelop them as with a mantle before he is done with them and the curtain falls.   In *Maria Stuart*, John Knox is the one personage untouched by this dramatic irony.   In his case Björnson waived his claim to take poetic liberties, for Knox was to stand forth at the close with the poet's ardent words on his lips, and declare himself, as representative of the people, to be Mary's political heir.   The hard fighting in *Sigurd Slembe*, the wild passions in *Maria Stuart*, terminated in sacred song. In both dramas the action was brought to a climax which permitted of their ending, the one in Ingermann's crusaders' chorus, the other in the Presbyterians' mystic psalm.

It gradually came to seem as if the author's once rich vein had almost dried up.   His later tales, *Railway and Churchyard* and *The Bridal March*, showed no improvement on the earlier; one of the very last, *A Life's Problem*, was pure mannerism.   In spite of its fine qualities, *Sigurd Jorsalfar* was not to be compared to the earlier dramas.   The Second Part of *Arnljot Gelline* was inferior to the First, written years before.   It seemed as if no new ideas were germinating in Björnson's brain.   People began to ask themselves if it was to be with this author as it had been with so many, notably with more than one Dane, that before he reached the prime of manhood his voice was to be heard no more, because he did not possess the secret of restoring, renewing his strength.   It was evident that he had exhausted his original capital.   Was he incapable of supplying its place by new treasures? Like the young Viking about whom he has written one of his finest poems, he had stood at the helm after his victory over the old times and their leader, calling to those who were alarmed by his daring steering, "Have I your leave now?" He had leave now, and he did not know whither to steer.

Those years have left an indelible impression on my mind. It was with an extremely painful feeling that one compared the intellectual, and more especially the literary condition of Scandinavia with that of the rest of Europe. In the North one had the feeling of being shut off from the intellectual life of the time. We were sitting with closed doors, some brains struggling fruitlessly with the problem of how to get them opened. The look-out seemed hopeless. For 1864 had beaten at the door with its iron knuckles, and it had not opened; 1866 had knocked in vain; even 1870 with its mailed fist had only shut it the tighter. It was a door that opened outwards; it had to be opened from within.

For a number of years back an art had been cultivated in Denmark with growing success, the art of reading European literature and ignoring whatever in it was opposed to the accepted national idea of what was to be found in European books. With whole schools of foreign literature the cultivated Dane had almost no acquaintance; and when, finally, as a consequence of political animosity, intellectual intercourse with Germany was broken off, the main channel was closed through which the intellectual developments of the day had been communicated to Norway as well as Denmark. French influence was dreaded as immoral, and there was but little understanding of either the English language or spirit. In Denmark they looked to Norway as the land from which the literary renascence was to come; in Norway they looked to Denmark, as the land of an older civilisation, for trustworthy and searching criticism.

Among the most cultivated, upper-class Scandinavians, David Strauss and Feuerbach were discussed as they had been discussed among the most narrow-minded, middle-class Germans of the forties; Stuart Mill, Darwin, and Herbert Spencer were scarcely known by name; positivism and evolution were powers which Scandinavia did not recognise; nothing whatever was known of the development of English poetry between Shelley and Swinburne; and as regards French literature, the very newest fashion was the general condemnation of Victor Hugo and the romantic school, whom Heiberg, the dictator in matters of taste, had called a troop of brigands. There was not the faintest apprehension of the significance of the fact that the French novel and the French drama had long ago forsaken heroic and legendary themes, and were finding their material in the life going on around the author, which is the only life he can observe with his own eyes, and also the life which, better than that of any other time, he can study in himself. It was seldom that any Scandinavian dared to push aside the curtain which hid the present from view; it long seemed as if the literature of the North were to reap no benefit from all the scientific progress of the century.

And whilst all spiritual life was dwindling as a plant dwindles in a close, shut-in atmosphere, a general feeling of self-satisfaction prevailed. It was not joyful, boisterous self-satisfaction, for great misfortunes had saddened men's hearts and depressed their minds, although these misfortunes were looked on as utterly undeserved, as cruel, crying wrongs. It was a dull, quiet, self-satisfaction; men deluded themselves with the hope of a speedy redress of their wrongs, enjoyed the sympathy which a brave resistance had aroused, rested on their laurels, and fell asleep.

And while they slept they dreamed. The educated, and to a still greater extent the half-educated classes of Denmark and Norway dreamed that they were the salt of Europe. They dreamed that they were imparting new youth to the other nations by their idealism, their Grundtvigian and Kierkegaardian theories, their keen alertness. They dreamed that they were the power that *could* rule the world, though for some mysterious, incomprehensible reason they had for many years back preferred to eat humble pie. They dreamed that they were the free, mighty North, which was leading the cause of the peoples to victory— and they awoke in bonds, impotent, ignorant.

VII

IN the early seventies Denmark was stirred by a modern intellectual and literary movement, which in the last decade has produced a new school of poetry and criticism. The intellectual agitation was quickly transmitted to Norway. There original thinkers, under English and French influence, brought about a kindred movement among the younger men, and Björnson's writing soon showed that—as he himself has expressed it—new and rich springs had begun, after his fortieth year, to well up within him. It suddenly became evident that his productive power had received a fresh impetus. The modern world lay open to view. He had now got, as he once wrote to me, "eyes that saw, ears that heard." The ideas of the century had, almost without his being conscious of it, come into contact with his receptive poet's mind, and fecundated it. In those years he read greedily books in many different languages and of many different kinds. Norwegian historical criticism was perhaps what influenced him first. John Stuart Mill's tranquil greatness and noble tolerance made a deep impression on him; Darwin's wondrous hypothesis widened his mental horizon; the philological writings of men like Steinthal and Max Müller gave him a new view of religion, the literary criticism of men like Taine a new view of literature. The significance of the eighteenth century, the task of the nineteenth, revealed themselves to him. In a most interesting letter to myself he once touched on the circumstances which had influenced his youth, and on the traits in his character which pre-determined his change of opinions :—

"Under these conditions I was bound to become Grundtvig's prey. But although I can be led astray by any one, the thing does not exist by which I can be bribed. The day my eyes were opened I was off again. It may be my worst enemy who holds the truth in his hands; I am stupid and strong; but on the day that I catch sight, even accidentally, of the truth, that

very day I go over to his side.   Will you tell me if this is not
a nature easy to understand?   Should not Norsemen of all
others understand it?   I am a Norseman.   I am a man.   That
is what of late I have chosen to subscribe myself: Man.   For it
seems to me that with us at present this word is awakening new
conceptions in men's minds."

VIII

THE first important work with which Björnson broke a silence of some years was the drama *Bankruptcy*. It was a plunge into modern life. The hand which had wielded Sigurd's sword felt it no degradation to count Tjælde's money and set down the items of his debt. Björnson was the first Scandinavian dramatist who in all seriousness undertook to write the tragi-comedy of money, and this first attempt was crowned with undoubted success. Simultaneously with *Bankruptcy* he published *The Editor*, with its passionate satire on the state of the Scandinavian press. On these two followed, in quick succession, *A King, Magnhild, Captain Mansana, The New System, Leonarda*, new poems, a popular treatise on republicanism, and lastly, *Dust*, a thoughtful, beautifully written story.

In Norwegian conservative circles an attempt has been made to depreciate both Björnson's and Ibsen's productions of this period by stamping them as works written with a purpose. Where this accusation is justifiable it certainly carries some weight. The *purpose* is always related to some one or other of the interests or tendencies of the moment; sooner or later it becomes out of date, and it may in the long-run shorten the life of the book. But we must remember, first, that there are many other things about a literary work which are liable to become antiquated —its form, its ideas, its language; secondly, that sometimes, as in the case of *Don Quixote*, the purpose of the work does not in the least impair its vitality; finally, and this is the main point, that the formula "written with a purpose" has been far too long employed as an effective scarecrow to drive authors away from the fruit that beckons to them from the modern tree of knowledge.

The warnings against writing with a purpose, and the low esteem in which such writing is held, are due to acceptance of the Kantian doctrine of art for its own sake, which in France has been formulated into the watchword, *L'art pour l'art!* This doctrine (which, strange to say, has always been resisted in its one

sensible and valid application, namely, as a protest against the
imprisoning of art in a strait-waistcoat of conventional morality)
has long been applied in the North to the purpose of excluding
all contemporary thought from our poetry, drama, and romance,
under the pretext that questions of the day are out of place in
literature; literary art, like every other art, being its own end
and aim.

On one side we heard: "Poetry, literature, is not its own aim
and end; it must and shall respect morality"—morality in this
case being perfectly well understood to mean the conventions of
polite society. On another, as soon as a work appeared which
showed the influence of the ideas of the day: "Scientific poetry!
problem play! Ladies and gentlemen, true literary art has no
object and aim but itself."

The opponents of the new style were under the naïve delusion
that those older works which they lauded were devoid of any
tendency, because their tendency was exactly the opposite of that
of the new works. Or is it the case that there was no tendency,
no sign of any intention in these older productions? Look at
Arnljot Gelline, with its obligatory Viking-conversions, common
to all the neo-Norse literature of the day. Hardly had Oehlenschläger, Grundtvig, and Hauch discovered these old Vikings
and begun to rejoice in their unimpaired strength, than they set
to work to convert and baptize them. It was exactly as if they
could not hit upon anything else to do with them, so monotonously
did the conversions recur. Both Björnson and Richardt followed
this lead. There was also a distinct orthodox tendency in all the
peasant tales of the period. This keynote of orthodoxy was
struck in the second chapter of *Synnöve Solbakken*, with a plain
enough indication that it would be retained in all subsequent
delineations of Norwegian peasant life.

Therefore what is objected to is not purpose or tendency as
such, for that, until now, has never been held to injure literary
productions. The public had become as thoroughly accustomed
to the old intentions and tendencies as people become accustomed
to the air of a room which they never leave. What is now condemned under the name of purpose or tendency is the spirit of
the times. But the spirit and ideas of the times are for the epic
and dramatic poet what the circulation of the blood through the
veins is for the human body. All we have to require in the

interests of art is that these veins, whose blue tracery does not detract from the beauty of the skin, should not stand out black and swollen, as they do in the case of a diseased or furious man.

At a rare time, purpose shows itself too plainly in Björnson's writing—at a very rare time; and a purpose which does not become part of the flesh and blood of the work of art, but projects inartistically from the canvas, is not more excusable or better in Björnson than in any other writer. I have no great admiration, for instance, for the attacks on the State Church, standing armies, and the whole social order of a monarchy, made by the hero of the drama *A King*, immediately before he commits suicide. We feel that this is something which the author desires to have said; the intention is too glaringly evident. That charming story *Dust* also suffers from its author's inclination to be didactic. In his enthusiasm for the truth he is occasionally tempted to give too direct, too vociferous expression to it, not noticing that exactly by so doing he detracts from that artistic effect which it is his object to heighten.

But setting this question of intention aside, it can only be by purposely hardening his heart against it that a man with any taste for poetry can remain insensible to the fresh welling up of poetic inspiration throughout these works of Björnson's second period—second youth we might rather say. A burning love of truth has set its mark on him. What individuality there is in these books; what powerful appeal for truthfulness towards ourselves and towards others; what a wealth of new ideas on all subjects—state and society, marriage and home-life! What charitableness too; what sympathy with the men, like the King and the Bishop in *Leonarda*, who represent those institutions of society against which the poet's attacks are directed! Nowhere is this more strongly felt than in *A King*. The fundamental idea of this play is the simple and by no means novel one, that a constitutional monarchy is a transitional form of government, leading to a republic. The author's originality is shown in the choice of a standpoint, in his letting it be the King who attacks the institution of monarchy, because of the harm which his human soul needs must suffer from the very nature of such an institution. The character of the King is drawn with a sympathy, a warmth of feeling, which make him in the true sense of the word the drama's hero.

In *Bankruptcy* we have the appeal for truth on the lowest plane—as simple honesty in everyday, middle-class life. But the author's keen eye sees that honesty is not the simple thing it seems. Thus it is blamable in the business man to risk other people's money, and yet it is to a certain extent unavoidable that he should do so. The question turns on the fine boundary-line, on the point beyond which it is not permissible to venture.

In *The Editor* we have the demand for truth in a higher sphere, where it is an imperative duty to have it always before one's eyes, and where it is still more difficult to satisfy. In the commercial world the danger is that a man, beginning with self-deception, will proceed to deceive and ruin others. The temptation in the journalistic world is to conceal or deny the truth. Here, too, the thing is to a certain extent inevitable; for a politician can never tell or admit everything. It is a weakness in Björnson's *Editor* that its representative of journalism fails to represent adequately the difficulties of his profession, the casuistry it entails, the perpetual, unavoidable difficulties in which the editor of a daily newspaper finds himself involved; he is too much of the rogue. His opponent and victim, Halfdan, is, on the other hand, too much of the passive and patient sufferer to awaken any great interest. In this play Björnson plainly makes an attack on the ideal of cool invulnerability which we in these latter days, impelled by stern necessity, have set up for ourselves. He protests—on behalf of the child within us—against the doctrine that we are to be "hardened"; and there is doubtless reason in his protest; but the fact remains, that nowadays we have only a very qualified sympathy with public characters who succumb to the persecution of the press. The Christian ideal of the suffering martyr has in this case practically lost its attraction for the reading and theatre-going public; the demand is for men whom the spoken or written words of their adversaries are powerless to injure, who are not shaken by even a hurricane of abuse. I do not maintain that this is a natural taste, but there is much to be said for it.

A King thrashes out political questions, as *Bankruptcy* and *The Editor* did social ones. The problem is psychological. The author fights the King's inward battle with him, and lets him fail in his attempt to reconcile the demands of his nature with the demands of his position. Is the problem satisfactorily solved?

L

162 BJÖRNSTJERNE BJÖRNSON

Is the failure not too necessarily predetermined by the worthlessness of the King's past life and his weak character? The value of the play is not materially affected by the answer to these questions; it lies in the depths sounded, in the fresh charm of the love-story (remember the scene where everything the King looks at seems to quiver and tremble), and the sparkling flow of the dialogue.

In *Magnhild* and *Leonarda* the author faces a new modern problem—the relation of natural to conventional morality, of the law of the heart to the law of society. The doctrine proclaimed in *Magnhild* is propounded in the modest form of a question: Are there not immoral marriages, which it is the truest morality to annul? The lesson of *Leonarda* is perhaps the one we stand most in need of in the North, that of charity, of social and religious tolerance, a lesson which the author himself only mastered in his riper years. Within a short space of time Björnson has conquered a whole new region for his muse.

Magnhild is a work which, in its striving after realism, marks a turning-point in its author's career as a novelist. In some of its character-delineation we have a delicacy and strength to which he had never before attained. We could hardly have credited Björnson with the ability to represent such characters as Tande, the young musician, and the beautiful Fru Bang and her husband. And Magnhild's relations with these principal personages are as admirably described as they are correctly imagined. All the same, we feel that the author is moving in a sphere which is still rather strange to him, that of upper-class society life. It is curious that Tande, in his cowardly desertion of the woman he loves when she is jeered at by the mob, has the sympathy of the author, from the moral point of view.

The story has two radical weaknesses. One is the ambiguity in the presentment of Skarlie, one of the leading characters. He is intended to impress the reader as being a kind of monster, and yet we find ourselves perpetually taking his part against his big, ideally perfect wife. It is hinted to us most cautiously and discreetly that in the matter of sexual morality Skarlie is an utterly depraved person; yet none the less this monster of low sensuality, in his relations with his own wife, whom he has won by a not particularly perfidious intrigue, realises Ingermann's moonshine-ideal of Platonic affection between husband and wife, being humbly and gratefully contented with the permission to feed and clothe the lady. The other weakness lies deeper in the philosophy of the story. There is a good deal of old-fashioned mysticism in the treatment of the doctrine of man's and woman's "destiny," on which the story turns ; and, as is always the case with both Björnson and Ibsen, the mysticism is curiously blended with rationalism. The conclusion which Björnson apparently intended us to arrive at from reading the tale was, that for a woman there exist other ways to happiness and useful activity besides union with a man she loves. It is an opinion well worth supporting ; but from *Magnhild* many other and contradictory deductions may be drawn. The idea of the book is not clear. It forms the antithesis of *Married ;* there is far more distinctness and vitality in the execution than in the conception.

Leonarda, from the dramatic point of view not specially important, is one of Björnson's most poetic works. It certainly deserved a better reception in Denmark than to be rejected by the National Theatre, and played in a theatre of the second rank amidst foolish manifestations of disapprobation. Posterity will have difficulty in understanding the narrow-mindedness which displayed itself in much of the Danish-Norwegian press's vilification of this beautiful and pure work of art. In *Leonarda*, the author, with admirable ability, brings a whole succession of Norwegian generations before us, delineating the representative of each with the sure hand of a master, and making the great-grandmother, who (somewhat in the style of the grandmother in George Sand's interesting drama *L'Autre*) represents the long-scorned culture of the eighteenth century, pronounce the play's solemn Amen. With *Leonarda* the time not only of strong feeling, but of bold thought, had returned.

The opponents of Björnson's later style maintain that as long as he kept outside the sphere of burning questions and living ideas he was great and good, but that since he has begun to meddle with modern problems and modern thought he has fallen off, or at any rate has produced no artistically perfect work. The same judgment has been pronounced each time that a European author who had won the favour of his public by harmlessly neutral productions has suddenly shown his contemporaries that he is studying and judging them. Everywhere throughout Europe there are readers who prefer Byron's *Childe Harold* to

Don Juan; in Russia and elsewhere there is a highly refined public which prefers Turgueneff's first small tales, such as *A Sportsman's Diary,* to *Fathers and Sons* or *Virgin Soil;* in Germany many ladies and gentlemen lamented when Paul Heyse for a time gave up producing love-stories, and wrote *Children of this World.* It is true that in this his second period Björnson has not yet attained the uniform transparency and harmony of form which distinguish his earlier works; but it is neither just nor reasonable to assert because of this that he is falling off. A new, strong ferment of idea takes time to settle down, is apt to bubble over the edge; strong feelings and powerful thought have a certain fire and impetus, which render them less suitable for presentation in a perfectly smooth and polished form than the childishly innocent pastoral scenes of the idyll. All the same, what technical excellence many of Björnson's productions of the last few years display! The exposition of *Bankruptcy* is one of the best that has ever been seen in a theatre; the dialogue in *The Editor* is the best its author has yet written.

These two dramas, with which Björnson struck into the path which had been opened up by Ibsen with *The League of Youth,* turn on themes akin to that of Ibsen's play. In *The League of Youth* we have both a bankrupt and an editor. The bankruptcy is that of the reckless Erik Brattsberg; in Stensgaard's relations with Aslaksen's newspaper in the matter of the article that is first to be and then not to be printed, we have *The Editor* in faint outline. The editor himself is in some ways an older Stensgaard, the softer and more pliable elements of whose character can now only be traced in his wild fits of contempt for himself and others ; what remains, and forms the leading feature of the character, being that brutal indifference to the feelings of others displayed in the threat to Aslaksen that if he does not yield he "shall be in the poor-house before the year is out." And yet the whole tone and spirit of *The Editor* is much milder and more lenient than that of *The League of Youth;* here and there, there is even a touch of sentimentality. The play is, however, apprehended most accurately and completely when read as a great allegory. Halfdan, the eldest brother, who succumbs in the political and literary strife, is Wergeland, who, after a life of noble and spirited conflict, lay so long on a sick-bed, an even more impressive and poetic figure there than he had been during his long life-battle.

The younger brother, who undertakes to carry on the work, is Björnson himself—"there is strength in Harald." And the third brother, who is a peasant, and his wife, who, without appearing on the scene, plays so important a part, represent the Norwegian people. This drama, like *Leonarda*, looks backwards as well as forwards; it has a wide horizon.

Henrik Ibsen is a judge, stern as one of the old judges of Israel; Björnson is a prophet, the herald of a better time. At heart Ibsen is a true revolutionary. In *Love's Comedy*, *A Doll's House*, and *Ghosts*, he strikes at marriage; in *Brand*, at the State Church; in *Pillars of Society*, at the upper middle-class. Whatever he attacks is shattered by his weighty and searching criticism, and we catch no glimpse beneath the ruins of any new organisation of society. Björnson is a reconciliatory spirit; there is no bitterness in his warfare. April sunshine plays over his works, whilst Ibsen's in their sombre earnestness lie in deep shadow. Ibsen loves the idea, the psychological and logical consequence—which drives Brand out of the Church, Nora out of wedlock. Corresponding to this love of the abstract idea in Ibsen, we have in Björnson love of humankind.

IX

EVEN in his youth Björnson began to take an active part in politics, and he may in so far be said to have worked all his life with the same conviction, that he has never ceased asserting and endeavouring to secure the independence of Norway in its union with the larger neighbour country. In every part of Europe, except Scandinavia, Norway is looked on as a country ruled by the "King of Sweden." Even those who have retained from their school-days a certain impression of Norway being itself a kingdom, involuntarily think of the country as a province of Sweden; and every time that a misunderstanding occurs between the King and the Government on one side and the Norwegian Parliament on the other, we see Norway mentioned in the European newspapers as a sort of rebellious Ireland. This circumstance is a natural result of the fact that the King resides in Stockholm, and that the foreign policy of the kingdom is directed by a Swedish minister; but it shows how necessary it is that Norway should be on its guard against any further attempts to place it in a subordinate position as regards either Sweden or the ruler of the united kingdom.

It is well known that ever since 1814 the house of Bernadotte has from time to time endeavoured to bring about the amalgamation of Norway with the neighbouring kingdom, and to restrict the constitutional privileges of the Norwegian people; and the Norwegians on their side have been prompt to espy a new danger in every attempt made to knit the countries together in closer political union. As early as 1858, Björnson, as the young editor of the *Bergensposten* newspaper, opposed such an attempt, and it was partly due to his action that the members of Parliament for Bergen who had voted for a closer Customs Union (Zollverein) between Sweden and Norway were not re-elected. In 1859, as editor of the Christiania newspaper, *Aftenbladet*, he vigorously defended the right of Norway to resist the appointment of a Swedish Statholder. In 1866-67, as editor of the *Norsk Folkeblad*, he was one of the strongest opponents of the so-called "Union Bill," the object of which was to unite the two kingdoms more closely. Ever since the dispute broke out between King Oscar and the Norwegian Parliament on the subject of the King's "absolute veto," and more especially since a visit to America in 1858 gave him the opportunity of studying American popular eloquence, Björnson has been one of the most influential political leaders in Norway. He is also probably the greatest popular orator of Scandinavia. It deserves to be noted and remembered that never, during his struggle for the independence of Norway, has he allowed himself to be provoked into saying a thoughtless or slighting word of Sweden; he has always declared his warm affection for that country.

No notice of Björnstjerne Björnson is complete unless it deals with him as journalist and public speaker; but to do this it would be necessary to have at hand a complete collection of his newspaper articles and important speeches. All the different stages of development he has passed through could be studied even better in them than in his literary works, and for this reason it is desirable that such a collection should be published during his lifetime. Much immature and foolish writing would probably see the light, but also enough of what is admirable and instructive to fill many volumes. Few wield a polemic pen like Björnson, and few have his gift of writing popularly without writing diffusely.

But it is as an orator that Björnson shows himself to us most unreservedly and entirely. In this capacity he is a great, genial agitator. When I try to picture him to myself in the situation which suits his inmost nature best, I see him standing on the platform at a public meeting, tall and broad-shouldered, towering above thousands of Norwegian peasants, swaying the silent multitude around him by the mighty tones of his voice and his irresistible devotion to the truth, greeted by a storm of jubilant homage the moment his voice ceases.

The Norwegian and Danish nations, who for so many hundred years were politically united, who build intellectually on the foundation of the same old literature, who to this day have one and the same written language and form one reading public, are also one in their attitude towards the great intellectual questions of the day. The modern Norwegian and Danish literatures, written in the same language with immaterial differences of dialect, are, under two names, in reality only one literature. The same desire for the spread of full, free, modern enlightenment which inspires Björnson in Norway, inspires the younger generation in Denmark. Each from his own side, we are working at the cultivation of the one literary field.

Who knows! Perhaps the same thing may happen that happened with the covering of the bare hillside in *Arne*: when, after many fruitless endeavours, the day comes at last on which the heather gets one eye, and the birch its whole head, up over the top of the rocks, they discover, with many a "Well, now, who would have thought it?" of glad surprise, that there is on the other side of the high plateau a whole wood—fir and heather and juniper and birch—standing waiting. They are met by the work that has been done from the other side.

"Yes, this is what they call success," said the juniper.

INDEX

(HENRIK IBSEN)

INDEX

(BJÖRNSTJERNE BJÖRNSON)

LaVergne, TN USA
28 April 2010
180880LV00003B/14/A